SINK OR SWIM

By

Daniel P Stimson

SINK OR SWIM

Author: Daniel P Stimson

Copyright © Daniel P Stimson (2023)

The right of Daniel P Stimson to be identified as author of this work has been asserted by the author in accordance with section 77 and 78 of the Copyright, Designs and Patents Act 1988.

First Published in 2023

ISBN 978-1-915492-62-3 (Paperback)

Book cover design and Book layout by:
    Maple Publishers
    www.maplepublishers.com

Published by:
    Maple Publishers
    Fairbourne Drive, Atterbury,
    Milton Keynes,
    MK10 9RG, UK
    www.maplepublishers.com

A CIP catalogue record for this title is available from the British Library.

All rights reserved. No part of this book may be reproduced or translated by any form or by any means, electronic or mechanical, including photocopying, recording or by any information storage and retrieval system without written permission from the author.

The views expressed in this work are solely those of the author and do not necessarily reflect the views of the publisher, and the publisher hereby disclaims any responsibility for them.

Dedicated to Donna

You have been my best friend for over 30 years and quite simply the centre of my universe. Thank you for the love and unwavering support you have given me every time I have had another 'bright idea'. You are my world.

Preface

Everyone starts every day with the same, twenty-four hours; a chance and a choice. How you use that opportunity is up to you……Sink or swim; yes or no! left or right.

So why have you picked this book up? I'm guessing you are looking for some 'self-help' and guidance to take you somewhere you're currently not. You want to get there/somewhere else, but don't know where to start. Or maybe you're a swimmer and have just mis-read the title of the book (I do that all the time, it's fine, I'll give you a refund). Oh, and a bit like writing books, I can't swim either! Well, if the former is correct, please be warned that this is not, I repeat *Not,* a self-help book (the clue is in the title), but it is a 'help' book. If, and it's a big if, you use the information, understand, and more importantly 'action' the processes set out in the coming chapters, it is definitely a 'help' book.

As you read this book you will discover that I'm a fairly logical, methodical individual, and that this book is my attempt (in my simple way) to rationalise how my brain works and to hopefully 'help' you to understand how your brain works too. Plus, to learn from my mistakes and understand the clear, relentless, 'goal driven' mindset you will need to get you to where you want to get to in life.

Let's be clear: life is hard, and we all need some help to move our own personal needle in the right direction. I'm hoping that this book can do that for you via a three-pronged attack on the issue. The book is set out into three distinct sections:

First section: Me and my brain.

Second section: The lessons via a story/fable.

Final Section: The 'how to' section where I show you how to apply the lessons.

YUP! You read it right, this is '**Not**' a self-help book! I'll set out what I mean by this later in the book, but essentially you have to walk your own path and this book just gives you the route map and guidance. How you interpret and use the information is up to you.

SPOILER ALERT!! Let's get this big one out of the way early.

Where you find yourself today is a product of your decisions and is therefore completely your fault! If you had control over the decision, you got what you deserved.

There I have said it. Now you need to deal with it!

Along with not being a self-help book, what this book is also not is 'The Answer' or 'The Secret' to life's eternal question 'why am I here?'. No, that's not in my gift, unfortunately. If I could give you that gift I would, I promise, but I can't. This book will also not give you the key to a pain free, stress free life of abundance. And, moreover, it certainly will not give you the motivation to achieve your goals. These things are in your gift, under or within your control and the only way you'll get these desirable outcomes is by bucking up, getting your hands dirty and putting in the work.

There are no short cuts…none! You must be prepared to 'out work' the old you and you will at least get somewhere.? It may not be where you want to be, but it also won't be where you are currently. That I can promise, but it's up to you and only you.

Furthermore, this book is also certainly not rocket science and definitely not brain surgery. It is not the reinvented wheel, the new grey, better than sliced bread or the new dawn. (I seem to be telling you what this book isn't more than what it is! I was never a good salesman!).

It is, however, 'real' and it does work. So, if that doesn't bother you or offend you (it might even inspire you) and sounds something like 'a plan' then read (or listen) on. (Side note – it could also be cure for insomnia though!)

Once you've read the book, taken in the lessons and understood the system set out in the book, you'll be in the position to fend off the questions from your work mates, insomniac friends, and your family: 'how do you fit it all in?', 'where do you get the energy from?', 'I didn't know you could do that!', and 'what's your secret?'. You'll be able to hand them a copy of this book so they can find out for themselves.

Introduction

My name is Daniel I'm 55 (as of 2022) I'm dyslexic and I see myself as different, you'll understand why I see my-self this way as you read this book so I won't spoil it for you.

To a certain degree I believe my brain works differently to most other people's, but maybe it actually works exactly the same? I don't know, because I can only describe how my brain functions. I think I have always seen myself as 'different' anyway. Moreover, I see my inner 'chimp' (Dr Stephen Peters) mind as very strong and very different to other people's too.

So, what makes me so different (in my mind anyway)? I've been told by a professional clinical psychologist, physiotherapists and behavioural specialist that I'm an unusually equalled balance of introvert and extrovert. I'm a living, breathing, human dichotomy...literally.

Let me briefly explain what I mean:

- I overthink things, but also make impulsive, rash decisions.
- I love my own company but play to the crowd when in a group - I'm an absolute show off.
- I'm fascinated with the numbers and metric, but at the same time I can be creative, carefree and artistic.
- I get concerned about how over-confident I am.
- I plan and strategize, but also daydream at the same time.
- I'm OCD in some aspects of my life, and a complete mess and disorganised in others.

I hope by now you are getting my point. I'm on the outer- extremes of personality traits that are used to define you as a person, and I don't fit into the stereotypical groups because I'm basically both sides of the same coin. I'm 'all-in' or not interested.

This list only covers a few of my idiosyncrasies. I could go on and on about the opposing aspects of my odd personally and how I function, but you will probably stop reading and think this is written by some self-serving nut job. But I also don't care what you think, so, I will also tell you that I have an unwavering ability to love deeply, care for others, and would ultimately die for certain people, but in equal measure I have the power to hate, be cruel and borderline Narcissistic to others. I am, in my own mind, a living contradiction - the classic puzzle wrapped up in an enigma (I'm not sure what that means but it sounds right).

So why does this make me special, I hear you ask? Well, I'm pretty sure you are saying that this just makes me normal and this is how everyone's mind works. This may be true, but the key difference between you and me is that I've come to understand how my brain works, analyse it and use that knowledge to create my system for working out life's puzzles, and when needed, using the systems for achieving things, or for changing or moving where I am in life and taking responsibility for where I am. But also drawing a line in the sand at any given time and committing to the process of change. One such commitment was to write the system and the processes in this book. Case in point: I'm a dyslexic person who thought writing a fucking book was a good idea 'for goodness' sake'!

So, what is this system? Why is it important? Who is it aimed at? Moreover, why should you care and want to read the book? Well, those are relevant and important questions. And to answer them simply in one sentence, I would suggest:

The base principle is; a system set up to organise a chaotic mind and give it some semblance of structure and order, by setting out a route map to follow.

The system is important, to me anyway, because I know my mind is chaotic and unstructured naturally, plus my inner 'chimp' is strong and it needs controlling. So I needed a robust system, based around logic and order, that provides a structure and a blueprint for me to follow. Without the blueprint I would just be floundering in open water with a boat load of annoying chimps for company, and no one wants that!

Who is this book aimed at? Well, the truth is anyone, or everyone with a similar personality to mine. Anyone who wants to take responsibility for who they are, where they are in life and draw a line in the sand, or just to move on up to something better and a more fulfilling happier place in life generally. Does this sound like you? If it does, read on.

I hate the term 'BETTER VERSION OF YOU', because ultimately, 'we are where we are'! Therefore, the current and past versions of ourselves are what we have created from our own decisions in life. So, the notion that this version is 'better' is pointless and self-serving, in my view.

My advice is buck up, crack on with the version of you that you currently see in the mirror, because it is the only one that counts. For better or worse, and definitely till death (well that's a sobering thought). But, for the purposes of this book, and so you can relate to the overview of the book, we will use that term. There, I've said it. This book will help you become a better version of you.

Spoiler alert: the term 'Better' is subjective, so if you become a 'Bitter' version of you...sue me.

The brutal reality of life is that you are where you are meant to be. You have got 'you' to where you currently are, through your decisions. That is to say, **if** they were in your control, then you are responsible for the outcome.

Every outcome in your life is directly related to a decision or choices you made. Because guess what? you made those choices and decisions, no one else. You said yes or no to the offers, you turned left when right was an option. No one else but you! If you disagree with this statement, stop reading now and throw this book in the bin. The brutal truth is that it's on you 100%, and once you get over that fact and take responsibility for your life, you'll be in a much better place. So, get over it and move on because you got the life, wife, job, and even health that you asked for.

We all see the world differently, and that's the quirk in the matrix of life that makes it interesting. We have our own personal perceptions of this world, constructed from our experiences and created from the learning patterns we are exposed to from an early age. Our own reality is affected and directed by these influences and experiences. What we need to do is re-wire and re-frame our learning system to create a new path and therefore a new learning experience, and thereby 'grow' and move the needle of our own life. Hopefully, this will be in a positive and enjoyable way. But ultimately, you guessed it, this is, again, ultimately up to you.

Please note: Some people like pain and misery and if that's you, crack on because I'm not saying what makes me happy is what makes you happy. In fact, liking, enjoying or accepting pain is (for me most definitely) a positive attribute to creating that life changing mindset.

Spoiler alert: Life is fucking cruel, hard, mean, nasty and it doesn't care that you want to be happy!

So how will this book help you? Good question! Please be aware, this is how my brain functions and how I learn. The book is based on my funky personality, how I see the world and meet it head on! It may or may not work for you and, may also not be how your brain functions from a learning perspective. Importantly, I reiterate, this book is not the secret to life, it's not the answer to everything it's just 'what I do' and 'how I do it'. It certainly is not ground-breaking or the wheel re-invented. It's just how my brain functions best if I want to change what I'm doing or where I'm at in life. No tricks, no bullshit: just a system and an honesty about who is in charge of the bus. If you want it to help you then get on the fucking bus and take charge of the decisions that affect the direction it is traveling in.

(Caveat alert! not a real bus this is just a metaphor for your life. Please do not attempt to drive a real bus, unless that's your job).

When I want to understand a process or just get my head around something new, or retain information, I've found that my brain functions best when I can give it analogies and stories to create a picture around the narrative. So, here's one I made earlier.

Texas Hold'em

I love the game of poker and life is very much like a game of poker. No one knows what hand you've been dealt (unless you show them), and you get to play your hand any way you want to. The best hand doesn't always win, and a poor hand doesn't always lose. More importantly, having a poor hand just means you have to work harder to win by bluffing or showing strength when you're actually in a weak position. The winner is the one who played the hand he/she was dealt with the most skill.

This was never more apparent than when I once played online poker and covered the cards I was dealt. This meant I had to effectively 'pretend' what cards I had. During the tournament I made my bets; raised or folded depending on how the other players reacted to my strategy. The outcome was, after around 4 hours or so of pretending what hand I had, I won the tournament and around $250! Not bad for playing blind the whole time.

Furthermore, and interestingly, when I looked back at my hand list online, I had folded a pair of Aces 4 times (one of the best starting hands in poker) and a pair a Kings 3 times. You see, it is not your hand that defines the outcome, but it's how you play your hand that counts. Poker is a bit like life in that regard, it's how you react to the situation you are presented with that determines the outcome, not the event itself. It's your call (excuse the pun!).

As with all games you must have a plan at the start, then implement the plan as the game develops. My book is the 'plan'. It won't mean you win but, it will give you much better odds.

As you've probably guessed, this is my first attempt at writing a book, it's my attempt at writing down what I see as the key fundamentals in achieving 'success' in life. But before I start, I thought it best for you to understand what I see as the unique workings of my mind that brought me to wanting to write this book in the first place.

I hope you enjoy the book. Obviously, it is written in way that would appeal to me as a dyslexic: short, simple, easy to read, and uncomplicated. You don't need to be dyslexic to read this, but it might help if you are or at least think like me.

Oh, one last point of note…this is not a book about being dyslexic - it's just written by won.

Spoiler alert: I know… 'one'! Those listening to this as an audio book you are not in on that joke…sorry!

Contents

Where It Started 14

Fit For 50 23

Sink OR Swim (The Story/Parable)

    1. On The Beach 29

    2. Sandcastles 48

    3. The Swimmer 54

    4. The Crab 62

    5. The Golfer's Mindset 66

    6. The Surfer 71

    7. The Yachtsman 79

    8. The Fisherman 86

    9. The Café 97

Lessons Learnt 104

Applying The Principles 106

How To Start 110

Motivation 118

My 14 Rules For Success 125

Curve Ball Thought 142

Final Thoughts 144

Quotes I Love 149

Your Next Chapter 151

About the Author 152

Where It Started

My own story started as an 8-year-old boy being told I was dyslexic and then dealing with the fallout from that discovery. Honestly, I have to start here because I don't actually have much of a memory of my childhood before this point.

Truth be told, if I had been able to understand the ***gift*** I had been given instead of the curse or disability I thought it was, my journey would have been so much simpler. Not easier, just simpler. Life is tough, whether you're gifted, talented, poor, wealthy or just born average. Life is hard, it's just how you deal with your version of 'hard' that counts.

If I could have spoken to the 8-year-old Daniel, when he was given the diagnosis 'you're dyslexic, son', I would have told him he has a **'*Superpower*'**, not a curse, and he just needed to understand how to harness that power. But real life is not that simple. There was no one there at the time to alter my perception, and the news was devastating.

So now I call it my superpower, but let's be honest about it, it's really just me re-labelling and re-framing dyslexia to take ownership of it.

I think it's really important that everybody who has a label is able to reframe that label to actually work to their advantage. Dyslexia, whether it's described as a disability or an ability, whichever way you want to look at it, it's really just someone else's perception of where you sit on the spectrum relating to your academic ability - your ability to read and write. Your cognitive ability - your ability to spell or add up. Simple as that is, or sounds, it's just someone's decision on where you sit on the spectrum of capability.

There has been a lot of noise lately around the 'Gift or Superpower' tag actually being a reverse negative. Some people are very angry that well-meaning celebrities are advising and heralding the positive aspects of Dyslexia and this is, in some way insulting to us 'ordinary people, and 'we' should all accept that learning difficulties, such as, dyslexia or dysphasia are not 'gifts', but a curse, and should not be looked at in any other way.

My view, and more importantly my response to this is; stop being a victim and get a fucking grip. Play the hand you're dealt and reframe your situation to see the advantages rather than the disadvantages and negatives. One of my 'Gifts' is that I can see around problems (hence my system), and that is something I use to my advantage. I don't accept not being able to spell the word 'advantages' as an obstacle. For me it's about using the positive aspects of dyslexia. But that's just me, and I can't speak for other people or where they are in their own life. However, I would strongly advise that anybody who has been given a label such as dyslexia re-frames it and re-labels it to take ownership of it.

Your future happiness depends on it!

That being said, this is not a book about dyslexia, this is a book about how I manage my life and how I structure my life when there is a journey to be made. This is not by any means specific to people with 'abilities' such as dyslexia. It is just as relevant for academically normal individuals as it is for individuals, such as me, with a label, which some people call dyslexia.

The process of re-framing the situation you find yourself in is one of the most powerful actions you can take. This book (and we will delve into the process of re-framing later) is the tool you need to undertake that process. If you are going to stride out into the world as the 'new you', then- 'fucking own it'! That starts with re-framing how you see yourself.

So how do you use the book, and who is it aimed at? Good question! Firstly, it's aimed at anyone wanting to start a journey but doesn't know how or where to start. Secondly, the book is set out to create a narrative to enable you to pick it up, put it down and re-read it at any time, and to use it as a reference point and guidance tool. I'm hoping you will pass it on to others and spread the message of the journey's rules as a template for anyone to follow. At the very end of the book, I set out my 14 rules for success. Also, there are a multitude of mantras, systems, and motivational quotes that could be used to suit your own personal needs and requirements. In no way is this an exhaustive list, it's just **my** list. Take it use it, adapt it and add to it as you see fit. There are no 'secrets' (as some books profess to enlighten you to some mystic 'secret' for success and happiness). I would like to say they are actually 'common sense', but the only trouble with that is the common sense is it's **not** very common.

So, let's just call them for what they are: My 14 rules for starting a journey that may end in success if you can stick to the programme. Bit of a mouth full that! Sink or Swim sounds better in my opinion.

Looking back to how the whole thing started, we have to go back to 1974 when my mother was told '*your son is just thick*'. And so, it began. The path of being labelled in a society that only saw a narrow spectrum of academic intelligence as a measure of an individual's ability to function in a 'normal' society (whatever that is). I'm not sure much has changed in 47 years except that kids get more help to conform to the basic academic standard. But labels are still labels and the dyslexic mind is still a 'disability' not an ability for seeing the world differently.

That being said, every individual still has the opportunity to react to their situation in any way they want. You can sink or swim. Your choice.

The great stoic philosophers set out the system of controlling your reaction to situations by placing uncomfortable tasks to condition your mind to outside influences and, I must say they have been a strong driver in my own mindset development. Great mindset motivational quotes such as *'Control the controllable'*, *'See it, believe it, achieve it'* and *'get comfortable with being uncomfortable'* are all very inspirational. However, as a gentle, quiet and slightly scared 8-year-old having a *'Fuck you! Go hard or go home'* mentality is very difficult. And, unsurprisingly, it took me over 4 years to develop even a sniff of this mindset. Suffice to say it was beaten out of me rather that coaxed!

My early upbringing was a very standard white, British, middle class one. I was the middle child of three. My father was a dentist and my mother, a former air hostess with Pan Am, was a stay-at-home mum, bringing up 3 children. My older brother and younger sister were both what you would call academically normal (my brother more 'gifted' but don't tell him I said that).

At the age of 11, I was sent to a boarding School just outside Christchurch in Hampshire, to enable me to have 'special educational lessons' due to my dyslexia. This was not a happy time in any shape or form, apart from my love of sport.

My school life was not a happy one to say the least. I was bullied and suffered mental and physical abuse whilst at school, and this is a chapter of my life that doesn't sit well with me. It shaped me (without question), however it is not a journey that any child should have to face to enable them to grow. But, without this aspect of my life I wouldn't be who I am today, so there is a real contradiction and dichotomy in the situation I experienced. Maybe that's for another day.

On the plus side though I found sport, and this was the only thing that saved me and was, without question, the most significant catalyst for my strong mindset development. In a rugby playing boarding school, only the strong survived and rugby was the battlefield. I could not read or write, but I could run like the wind, sidestep and drop kick, which made me a valuable member of the team. I eventually (once I had learnt the rules) played fly-half, number 10, the General on the field. This is a position of control, skill, timing and organisation! You had to be vocal and strong minded toward your teammates and tactically aware and adaptable in response to the opposition. The parallels for life are not lost on me. Sport, and moreover rugby, saved me and in some respects made me.

To put my dyslexia into context, I struggled to read and write at the age of 9 and 10 years old. I would write most letters backwards and could not concentrate for more than 1 minute on any aspect of reading or learning. My reading age at 9 was probably closer to a 5-year-old (there were no audio books or computer spell checking back then). School life in the 1970's was hard, especially if you struggled to read, write or concentrate. The term 'thick' or 'dunce' were terms used regularly and the remedial class was the place you spent your school days being watched (marshalled by the PE master) and just staying out of trouble.

Still today, the basic measure of a child's academic ability is reading, writing and arithmetic. In the seventies, dyslexia was not a consideration in respect of a child's special needs. So, you can see that I was swimming up hill, against the tide, in a system that was not sympathetic to my needs. My mother, however, saw that I was not 'thick' and to cut a long story short, I was sent off to boarding school to get special learning help and the academic support and help I needed.

At around 13 years old I had one of those 'light bulb' moments. I was told un-ceremonially (by my boarding school form teacher) that:

'Daniel you'll never amount to much and you should just accept that your brother is the achiever in the family. You should just keep your head down and make the best of it and try and keep out of trouble. If you're lucky you won't end up on the government unemployed statistics.'

This was my 'Oh right, thanks for that but...fuck you!' moment. I remember it like it was yesterday and I know some of you will say 'oh he was trying to motivate you'. No, he wasn't, trust me on that one. But it did set me onto a path that changed my complete outlook on life to what I describe as my 'I back ME, mindset'. As I quickly realised, the only person I could rely on was ME! Still to this day one of my 'mantras' is 'I BACK ME'. So, my journey pretty much started on that day and resulted in the driven, competitive, often relentless and most definitely stubborn individual you see today. The system's blueprint didn't happen straight away, but slowly over time I developed various systems for survival (mostly avoidance tactics due to my dyslexia). This book sets out the rules I have developed for one of my systems.

As I have grown and experienced life as an adult, a husband and a father, (foot note: during the writing of this book, I have become a grandfather too) I have come to realise that my system (though not ground breaking) works for every aspect of life. If you are willing to put the work in then anything is achievable...anything! You've just got to want it bad enough and work twice as hard to get it, or at least that's what I have to do.

At the end of my school life, after being kept back a year, I left with barely 2 O-Levels to my name (hint for millennials: O-Levels are now called GCSEs) both C grade, in Art and Religious Education. Not the greatest start to enter the world of work at 17.

Once I had left school, and was back home on the Isle of Wight, I struggled to cope with what I had experienced and was your quintessential 'angry teenager'. I did, however, eventually move into the world of work as an apprentice Stone Mason and I have worked on some of the most famous historic buildings in the country. During this time, whilst gaining my City and Guilds qualifications, I slowly developed my growth mindset, and my system for achieving my goals. This includes passing exams for my City and Guilds with distinctions as the top apprentice in the country (not bad for a thicky).

Then later, once I was married and a father with a mortgage (my wife working night shifts in the local hospital) I used my system to re-educate myself whilst in fulltime employment, by qualifying as a surveyor, gaining a Diploma from Reading University. This was a period that typified my 'I can do this' attitude. Trust me, for a dyslexic, two years of assignments, exams and being assessed with my peers without any concessions was tough. All this whilst working full-time, which meant writing dissertations and assignments at 2am. This was tough. Really tough. Looking back, I'm not sure how I actually did it, but that's where the system works, without question.

Looking back at this time, I can now join up the dots and see that it formed a significant part in my mindset and my confidence - in my ability to achieve anything. But it was another 15 years before I put the system to paper and started proactively applying the 14-point blueprint in other aspects of my life. One of which was to change everything, and ultimately brought me to this moment, in writing this book.

In no way do I profess to know everything there is to know about personal development or goal achievement, and I certainly don't have all the answers to solving life's puzzle. But that is (is it not?) half the fun of the adventure - not knowing what's coming next. The story you're about to read is my interpretation of how to use the tools you have, and believe me, you have all the tools you need there in front of you. You just need to learn what to use and what to lose from your 'toolbox' for the journey we all call...life!

In true support of my dyslexic mind, and hopefully to allow everyone to enjoy the 'story' element of the book, I've kept the passages short and to the point. Mainly because I can't concentrate for very long and it's not in my nature to waffle. I can, however, talk for England.

So 'Sink or Swim' is the title of the book (ironic in its very nature), that at 55 years old (as of 2022), I have decided to write, to share my system on survival and growth in a world that, in the most part, sets you up to keep you down. Or at least that's how most people see it, and therefore they never set sail on their journey in the first place. The book is a set of short 'lessons' to allow the reader to observe, from someone else's perspective, how to make that all important change in mindset and set a plan into action. I think we can all associate with looking at someone else's life and can see clearly where they are going wrong and their need to change, but seeing the same process in ourselves is very difficult. So, this book is here to help you use a different perspective to guide you on making those important changes in your own life.

Fit For 50

What qualifies me to tell you how to achieve your goals, move your needle and grow into the new you? I don't have a degree in psychology or sports science, I'm not an Instagram influencer, I don't have a successful YouTube channel to evidence my advice. No, you're right, I don't have any of these things...yet! 'Yet' is a powerful word. It allows you to keep an open mind and have hope on the outcome of any journey. 'I'm not there...yet.' Who knows, maybe my next chapter?

So, what does qualify me? Well, I'm just an ordinary guy with an ordinary life, a lovely wife, great kids and now grandchildren. The very fact that I am just an 'ordinary guy' is what should make this advice resonate in your mind. That is what makes this book so simple, yet genius in its approach. The fact that I am 'ordinary' means I know what it takes to achieve everyday things, in an everyday life, whilst still doing everyday things. By using a logical, methodical approach that works. Not to say if you wanted to be a billionaire or the next Prime Minister you couldn't use this system, because you could 100%, and it would work 100%. Though I feel most people, most ordinary people, (me included) just want a simple, healthy, stress-free, happy life where they can achieve 'reachable' goals to make small improvements to their life, relationships and their health. The 14-point system is applicable to every aspect of life and it is entirely in your gift to decide how, and to what degree, you apply the principles.

It all started for me, actually applying my system in a formal, structured approach, during early part of January 2016. I was 48 ½ year old and at this time in my life, a very unfit and unhealthy 'forty something', having once been a fit, healthy and active person in my younger years. Your classic skinny fat Dad bod had crept up on me. As a teenager, and in my 20s, I was fit and active. I played football, rugby, I ran, surfed and sailed. Then a knee injury in my 30s playing football stopped pretty much all sporting activities, apart from the odd round of golf.

A slow mission creep had manifested and I was now overweight, pre-diabetic, unfit and not very strong! Everything I wasn't in my 20s. In addition to this, in my mid 40s I was diagnosed with a neuroma (tumour) in my right arm. This meant that a portion of my right bicep had to be removed, and this most definitely contributed to the basic decline in my physique generally. I lost a lot of strength through inactivity and this was compounded by poor diet, stressful work life and poor sleep habits.

The light bulb moment was when my wife took a picture on her phone of me with my shirt off, after a walk on the beach (just for a joke). Well, the joke was on me because what I saw horrified me. The skinny-fat dad bod was real, and I was it in its purest form! I was not happy and at that moment, made the decision to change what I saw in the picture.

So, a drastic change of lifestyle and mindset ensued. I had absolutely no idea what I was doing! After 3 months of blindly running mile after mile, going to the gym and drinking protein smoothies, I realised I needed a plan. I remember being so cross with myself for not even entertaining the idea that my 'dyslexic system' for approaching life's challenges wasn't suitable for THIS life challenge. So, I sat down one cold, wet March day and I set out a fully planned system of achieving my goal of becoming thinner, fitter and healthier version of myself.

On the positive side, I naturally love research (don't ask me why, but I do). I love facts, figures, etc. and I want to know the numbers and the metric for everything (verging on the autism spectrum and most definitely obsessive) which, ironically was my saviour, because this was the basis for the plan to be put into action. As you already know, I had a system, though not written down or formalised, so I put it all down on paper and tried to work out a logical, methodical order of headings. The plan was being formulated.

A few tons of wastepaper later, the 14 headings had emerged. The blueprint was born, with a starting point: number one - Find your Passion. Or, in simpler terms, your reason for the journey (your 'why'). This was obviously easy for me because I had a picture of the unfit Dad bod I wanted to change.

The next part was to contextualise the plan So I visualised the end result (actually I googled fit men in their 40's – (Side note: Note to one-self delete search history it stops any awkward conversation with your wife or husband) printed off the picture and wrote down exactly what weight I was going to be, all my projected gym numbers for squatting; dead lifts; bench press etc, how fast I would run 5km and most importantly the date I would achieve all this by. I also wrote all my 'numbers' on the back of the image I printed off which was of a male physique that I liked and thought was attainable. I visualised the image every night (in the shower ... Good place to do visualisation.... Sorry if that's an image you may not be able shake!).

12.30pm 6th May 2017 - my 50th Birthday

My 'Get Fit For 50' campaign was born. And so began a systematic approach to health and fitness with specific target metrics and an end date. Putting the date down gave me a real sense of direction and focus, I was now driven by the ticking clock to achieve my goal. This was a huge motivation for me because suddenly I had told everyone this was what I was going to do, and being someone with a big ego I was not letting myself fail. Too many people have the ambition to achieve the outcomes but don't provide their mind with a specific target date and therefore get disillusioned when results don't happen. I really can't stress this bit enough, give yourself the exact date (even the time of day) and as long as it's realistic, your mind will be able to visualise the outcome and help you achieve it. This gives your mind a clear specific focal point to aim at.

In actual fact, not only did I achieve all my results I set out originally, in time for my 50th birthday, but I achieved much, much more.

Not only did I better I all of my fitness goals, but I also gained the following as an added bonus:

1. Increased testosterone (for a middle-aged man that's huge especially from a mental health perspective)
2. Improved sleep (I was basically an insomniac before, so 8 good hours sleep was perfect)
3. Increased energy (so I could work longer and go the gym more)
4. Improved focus - on all aspects of life
5. Improved skin (I always had dry skin from my stone masonry days)
6. Better posture (standing taller is better for confidence generally)

7. Clothes fitted better, and I looked physically better too

The above are just a few of the net gain aspects of eating healthier/ better and working out at the gym doing resistance training.

I also started a small fitness and wellbeing business - 'The Fit Mindset Code' - and competed in a fitness model, men's physique, body building competition, where I achieved first place in two categories. I've spoken at numerous events and have been invited into various businesses to talk about wellbeing and have become a monthly guest on a local radio show giving health, fitness and nutritional advice. From small acorns the mighty oak shall grow. You never know what opportunities will arise from our seemingly small decisions.

The decisions we make may seem innocuous initially, but these things grow and develop, and if you keep pulling at the thread, things happen. What started out as just 'getting fit' before I was 50, has now become part of my whole life, work and much, much more. When they say it's about a lifestyle change, they really mean it.

Some of my numbers:

Here are few of the numbers I achieved during my 'Get Fit For 50' campaign.

Body Fat %

2016 – 28% (pre-diabetic)

2019 – 6.5% (competition condition)

Weight

2016 – 13st

2017 – 11st (6th May 2017- my 50th Birthday)

2019 – 10st 4lbs (stage weight for the competition)

<u>Bench press (1 rep Max)</u>

2016 – 35 kg 1 rep

2017 – 75 kg 1 rep

2019 – 92.5 kg 1 rep

<u>5 Km run</u>

2016 – 32 mins 12 secs (1st Park run in March 2016)

2019 – 24 mins 17 secs

2020 – 21 mins 58 secs PB (lock down 1 2020, the positive aspect of COVID-19)

The numbers above may not break any records, but they are my numbers, I took the journey to achieving them and that's the point. You'll take your own journey and hit your own numbers. But enough of that.

As the boxer Mike Tyson once said, "Everyone has a plan until they get punched in the face"! This book Is the 'plan' after you get punched, to enable you to get back up and fight on!

Chapter One
On The Beach

Adam leant his back against the rough iron railing, pressed his heel against the opposite toe and flicked his grubby white trainers off. He stepped off the walkway onto the hot sand and moved swiftly (hoping no one saw him doing the hot sand chicken dance on the way), to the shade of the parasol area. He picked a lounger with a good view of the water and set his towel down. This was Adam's day off. A day off from the stresses of work and life generally, and he was determined to relax and enjoy the day on the beach in the warm afternoon sun.

After a sustained period of adjusting the towel and the head rest of the lounger, he finally settled and began to scan the shoreline. Adam was a mercurial 'people watcher'. He loved nothing better than amusing himself trying to guess who they were, where they were from, where they were going and what they were doing. He would often, for his own amusement, give them names and create a narrative around the situation, or their characteristics.

This was the first time Adam had been to this part of the beach, and on this particular day it wasn't too busy, so the choice of lounger position wasn't an issue. A few families, the odd dog walker, a father and son building sandcastles, a group of swimmers and some long-haired teak-tanned surfers. Out on the water were a couple kayaking and the odd boat on the horizon. A perfect selection of subjects for Adam to amuse himself with.

'I should come here more often', he thought to himself as he settled down into the lounger. He scanned the immediate vicinity and there were a few families, a body builder oiling his tanned muscular physique with way too much care (so Adam thought), but then Adam's gaze found an old couple sat on the loungers near the beach bar. Adam's mind started to create the narrative that would define these two old timers.

'Umm let's see, I think they would be 'Doris and Ken', possibly retired, and they are obviously hiding from something or someone', he thought, as they shuffled around the lounger area fussing with their bags and a small pooch. 'Perhaps ex-bank robbers from the '60s, now in exile and still on the run from the law'. He laughed out loud as they looked up and glared at him. Adam looked away and covered his mouth in a vain attempt to stop his sniggering from being heard. He settled back down on the lounger and began to scan the shoreline again.

The beach itself was a beautiful stretch of golden sand with turquoise and blue ocean waves crashing on the shore. The large horseshoe bay was bookended by a pier at one end and small harbour at the other. On a clear day you could see north across the to the mainland, and just about make out the large city tower blocks and hotels that dominated the skyline. The sun would glint off the glass of the tower blocks and make them appear like jewels glistening in the hot sun.

Adam's attention came back to the father and son building sandcastles near the shore break, he watched intently as the young boy hurriedly dug the moat in front of the sandy construction.

SINK OR SWIM

'Dad it's working!', the boy shouted. 'Yes, son! Keep digging' he replied. The boy shrieked with laughter as another wave swished around their handmade excavation.

Adam's moment of nostalgia, remembering his own sandcastle building days as a child, was broken by a loud shout from the water. A surfer catching a wave. Shouts of 'WOOOOHOOOO' and 'YEAH DUDE' came from the group on the beach, waxing their boards in readiness for the rides to come. The surfer kicked up the board's tail and sat perfectly back down on the back of the crashing wave, flicked his long, wet hair out of his face, and began to paddle back out.

'Wow, that's soooo cool', Adam thought. Further out, past the waves breaking, the kayakers were paddling across the bay. They seemed to effortlessly glide across the water, then, like a spear being thrown, a paddle would plunge into the water and the small craft would spin on a sixpence and change direction. Adam couldn't quite make out what they were talking about, but it seemed that they could see something in the water. With the paddles resting on the gunnels of the kayak, the small crafts just drifted for a while. As the two tiny boats bobbed about, a large fishing boat powered past them causing them to steady themselves in the wake. Far from being alarmed by this interruption to their morning on the calm sea, they seemed to enjoy the rough rollercoaster ride on the choppy waves created by the boat's wake.

But this was a day to chill and relax, not a day for kayaking or surfing, Adam thought to himself. So hard, full-on relaxing is what he was going to do. He leant back into the lounger, put his arms behind his head, crossed his legs and closed his eyes. As Adam slowly began to drift off, he was aware of his chest rising and falling as he breathed in and out. He could feel the warm sun on his face and a light warm breeze on his toes. 'Perfect!', he thought.

This moment of perfect tranquillity was short lived though, as a dark shadow appeared over his face and then Adam heard the words 'Three quid mate', a booming voice said.

Adam opened one eye. 'Sorry?', he quipped sharply.

'Three quid for the lounger', the man replied.

'Oh right, sorry'. Adam quickly scrambled around in his jeans pockets and pulled out a crumpled £5 note and handed to the large, imposing, shadowed figure.

'Thanks mate, two quid change', handing him the cold coins.

Adam took the coins and popped them onto the towel, shuffled about and tried to look as if he wasn't flustered by the interruption to his snooze. He propped himself up onto his elbows put one hand up to shade his eyes from the sun and looked out to sea.

Adam's gaze quickly fell back on the group of surfers rubbing their boards. He noticed there was an older guy just sat with his board on the sand, watching the waves. He seemed to be in a trance, just staring out at the water. Not moving just sitting and staring.

'He's watching the sets', a voice from behind him said. 'Excuse me?' Adam replied, twisting his head around and upside down at the same time, in an attempt to see who was talking to him.

'The guy...with the long board', said the voice behind him. Adam noticed that the old guy had a much larger board than the young surfers. 'Oh right...cool!' Adam responded.

It was the deck chair guy, still sat behind Adam, with a cold coke in his hand. There was a short, slightly awkward pause.

'Why?' Adam asked to break the silence.

The deck chair guy just laughed. 'If you need to ask, you've never surfed!'.

'No, you're right, I've never surfed', Adam confirmed.

'He's visualising the wave and counting the sets, so he can time his paddle out. It's all about seeing it and timing. The rest is just gravity.'

'Oh right, looks fun!' said Adam, not wanting to sound uninterested.

'Fun?!' said the deck-chair man, 'yeah it's fun alright, but it's also a way of life to these guys. They want to feel the ocean in their soul, feel its power through the soles of their feet and harness that power for as long as they can. Then, drop off the wave and do it all over again, until the sun sets', said the man, gazing out toward the waves.

Both men sat watching, transfixed, as the silhouetted, seal like, figures paddled out then dropped down the face of the wave. Like human dolphins playing in the wake of nature's tanker. It was mesmerising, fluid, poetic, and aggressive all at the same time. Adam could see the intensity on the surfers' faces as they furiously paddled below the lifting water, before the moment of truth when the board lifted and they pushed up with their arms, arched their backs and in one movement stood up. Then the expression of pure joy came over them, as they gracefully skimmed down the face of each wave, before kicking back over the breaking water to drop flat down on the board and paddle out again.

'What's your reason, young man?' The man asked.

'For what?' Adam replied.

'For being on the beach?' he asked.

Adam thought for a moment. 'Errr, to relax and forget about work and stuff, I guess. I'm not sure.'

The deck chair guy laughed. 'Well, if you really don't know why you're here then you're not here for right reason!' the man responded with a huff like laugh.

Adam was puzzled by the response and slightly annoyed. 'Why do I need a reason?' Adam asked.

'Why indeed?' the man replied. 'The beach is where '***it***' is my friend.' he added.

Adam was getting more than a little frustrated with the riddle-some answers that were being thrown back at him. 'Where *what* is? It's just a beach, right?' Adam said getting more annoyed as the question-tennis continued.

The deck chair guy took a sip of his coke and smiled. 'No, not just a beach to us man. But maybe just a beach to you!' he quipped sharply.

Adam's day up to this point had not gone well. In fact, his whole week had not gone well. If we are going to go there, his whole life had not gone well up to this point. Now, the fact that some strange old deck chair guy was getting all weird was about the last straw.

Adam was the middle child of a middle-class family. He was the perennial under achiever and always in the shadow of his older, smarter brother and always played second fiddle to the 'favourite' younger sister. To be fair, he never held a grudge against them, but he always felt that he was always in the shadows and his life had become completely in line with this mindset. Man and underachievement in perfect harmony.

Adam worked as a sales assistant in the local hardware store, which meant he had to pretend to know a lot about

DIY to sell materials and tools to people who knew even less about DIY than him. To say it was not his dream job was an understatement. However, it paid the bills and put food on the table.

Adam's girlfriend was a local highflying estate agent, so she worked most weekends which meant they rarely had days off together. I think deep down, Adam knew she liked it that way and, if pressed he would probably agree that it suited him too.

Adam's day had started around 4am, with his car alarm going off in the street. This then meant he slept in and had missed the 'click and collect' slot for his mother's groceries, which hadn't gone down well with his mother. Added to this, his car battery had gone flat, having left the interior light on whilst trying to stop the alarm going off at 4am. To cut a long story short, Adam was at the beach to forget his dull, uninspiring, 'flat battery' of a life, even if it was only for a few hours.

'I'm here to relax', he snapped. 'I'm here to (he shuffled into the lounger with intent), you know, relax!'

'Well, so important you named it twice!' the deck chair guy sarcastically replied.

'Very funny! What's so special about the beach? It's just sand, water and annoying deck-chair people!' said Adam, trying hard to impose himself on the discussion.

'I'll ignore the last bit, as I can see you're a bit stressed', the man said softly, seeing that Adam was getting slightly agitated.

The man moved next to Adam on the lounger. 'Well, let me see. The beach. What makes it a special place? Well, I'd say it's not just where the land meets the ocean, or where the sky sits waiting with bated breath for the morning sun as it slowly rises over the horizon, casting a golden seam of fire across the invisible, hazy line between heaven and Earth. No, not just that, but also where life lessons are taught, before life's adventure begins. Where plans are made and love is found, and sometimes lost. It's where dreams are made and journeys begin, and end. This, my friend, is what the beach '**is**''.

Adam sat open-mouthed, mesmerised by the image presented to him. 'Oh right, so not just hot sand and waves then?!' he said.

'I think, young man, you need some help' the man added.
'Help with what?!' Adam snarled.

'Help finding out *why* you're here…on the beach. Your purpose. But first let me properly introduce myself!' The man put out a large, sun-tanned hand out and Adam slowly placed his small, pale hand in the large, rough palm and shook it. The man's handshake was firm but not too firm to crush Adam's.

'Hi, you can call me Gruff' he said softly.

'Hello…Gruff? What sort of name is Gruff?' questioned Adam. He laughed. 'It's my nick name…it's a long story, a surfer thing. Nice to meet you, Adam.'

'How did you know my name?' he quizzed sharply thinking he was either a mind reader or some sort of stalker, he looked like neither, Adam thought to himself, somewhat confused.

Gruff pointed to Adam's store badge sticking out of the small, leather bag on the sand with '**Your store attendant is ADAM**' written in big orange letters.

'Oh right, yeah, my badge!' Adam laughed, somewhat relieved.

Gruff was probably mid-fifties, but with a physique that looked more mid-forties. Tanned, muscular (for an old guy), with long, scruffy hair loosely tied back with what looked like an old, faded flag. He was an imposing figure and looked from Adam's perspective somewhat 'weathered'. His leather flip flops looked like they were burnt onto his tanned, cracked feet. His long, faded, blue board shorts had seen better days, but it was 'a look' and kind of worked, Adam thought.

Gruff placed his big, rough, tanned hand on Adam's shoulder. 'So, let me guess. You're having a bad day after a bad week during a bad year? Am I right?' Gruff asked.

With a hang dog look 'More of a bad life, I think.' Adam replied.

'So why not change it?' Gruff asked.

'What, my whole life?' Adam scoffed in reply. 'How would that help?'

'Well, for a start you would have a chance to live a different life! And if you could choose it, perhaps you might be a bit more careful in choosing one you actually want to live?' said Gruff.

'You make it sound so easy! It's not, 'obviously' (Adam placed two hands up and pulled his index and middle fingers down, emphasising the word in a slightly condescending way), or everyone would be living their dream life and, quite plainly- they aren't!' he added.

'Who said anything about it being easy? I just suggested if you could get to choose your life, you should choose more carefully.' Gruff patted Adam on the shoulder again. 'But maybe you're not ready yet? Maybe you want to live your 'flat battery' of life a bit longer, just to make sure.'

'How did you know about the flat battery?' Adam asked, quizzically.

Gruff pointed to the garage receipt sticking out of Adam's bag, next to the name badge.

'Oh right.' Adam sighed.

Adam's gaze fell to the sand pushing up between his toes, and with another big sigh asked, 'Where would I start? I wouldn't even know where to start' he repeated desperately.

'You start at the beginning, Adam. That's where you start.' Gruff said warmly, patting Adam's shoulder again.

'THINK FAST' Gruff shouted, as he tossed a cold can of coke in Adam's direction. Adam managed to catch the cold can with one hand and his chest. The can popped up, like a slippery bar of wet soap, and with a second grab at it and a short juggle, it was under control.

Gruff laughed, 'Good catch! Let's take a walk' he said. As Adam opened the can, the exploding ring pull sprayed a cold, fizzy sugary liquid fountain straight into his face. 'Bleurgh! Nice, thanks!' Adam quipped. He wiped his face, took a sip and followed Gruff off down the beach.

Both men laughed as Adam wiped coke off his trousers and shirt. Gruff strode ahead across the hot, dry sand and didn't turn around as he asked, 'So, tell me about this dead pan, boring life of yours.'

The hot sand pressed though Adam's toes as he tried desperately to keep up, while also trying not to do the hot sand chicken dance again.

'Well, it's pretty dull really. I hate my job, plus I'm rubbish at it, my girlfriend would rather go to work than spend a day with me, my Mum thinks I'm useless and I have no future, and I would probably agree with her. Yup, that's about it really. Not much to write home about', Adam huffed out loud, to make a point of how shit his life was, expecting some kind of sympathetic response from Gruff. 'Oh, and I'm 35, which is like...middle aged!' he added, to ram the point home.

'Ok. so that's where you are today. Tell me, what do you dream of being? Not what you told your teachers when you were seven years old, coz that was then and this is now. The important thing is what floats ya boat now. What would get you up in the morning? What would make Monday exciting? What would you do for nothing, but still want to do it every day?'

'Apart from being a male model?!' Adam smirked.

'Yeah right, I can see that one.' Gruff tutted and shook his head looking at Adam's pasty 'Dad Bod' of a figure.

Adam thought for few seconds.

'Ok. Errr, not sure.... photography perhaps?' he replied 'I always liked photography at school, but I was told it wasn't proper career. Oh and stories, I love making up stories. Yup, stories and pictures.' he added confidently.

'Well, that's a start, but did you love it or just like it? Is it your passion?' Gruff asked, pressing his large hand onto Adam's chest on his heart. He then quickly wiped his hand on his shorts, to remove the residue of sticky coke from Adam's shirt.

'Well, yeah, I love taking pictures and I love seeing the image appear slowly, you know...the old-fashioned way? Developing in a dark room and then seeing the story emerge from the picture. It is like you can read the story any way you see it, and everyone sees it differently.' Adam replied excitedly. 'But I haven't picked up a camera for years.' he added.

'Ok, good. So, if you could photograph anything or anyone what, or who would it be?' Gruff asked.

'People, you know? Interesting people. Yeah definitely. It would be people.' Adam replied confidently.

'Not a proper career huh?! Tell that to David Baily or Lord Litchfield' Gruff snapped.

The two men continued to walk on.

'That's a good start. Let's see if I can help you find your path to achieving your dream of being a story telling photographer', said Gruff.

Adam puffed his chest out like a schoolboy who knew the answer to the teachers question in class, and a wry smile crept onto his face, that gave Adam a real sense of having achieved something important, but he was the only one that knew.

Gruff continued to walk, as the white foaming shore break waves washed up over his flip flops, up his legs, wetting the lower part of his tanned, sandy, fair-haired shins.

'I love the water' Gruff said thoughtfully.

'Why' Adam asked.

'I think I was a dolphin in another life' Gruff added.

Adam skipped alongside his new-found mentor and life Guru, like an exited puppy being trained by his new owner. As Gruff continued to stride on through the white foam on the shore, Adam kept glancing expectantly up, waiting for the next pearl of wisdom to fall.

Adam broke the silence. 'Ok, so what next? I can't just quit my job and just start taking pictures can I!' said Adam, firmly.

'No, probably not, but happiness in life is a strange one Adam. Your happiness is your responsibility, it's a personal choice. And more importantly, it is your fault if you are not happy. It's your responsibility to make sure you get to where you want to be in life to be happy!

'My fault! How the fuck is it my fault?' Adam said, with arms out wide.

'You see, Adam, the key is knowing what makes you happy, what gives your life meaning, and then moving towards it. You've got to know where you're going before you start any journey and, without question, you've got to be able to imagine yourself reaching the destination too.' Gruff stated sharply, hands placed behind his back in what Adam noted as a somewhat of a 'teacher' pose.

'You've gotta be able to see yourself doing what you want to do, because if you can't see it, who else will?' Gruff added.

'Ok, so let's say I say "Yes, I'd like your help", how's this going to work? Are you like Mr Miyagi or something?' Adam asked. 'You know, wax on wax off!' he added.

'I'm not sure about that, and I'm certainly not going to ask you to wax my car!' Gruff laughed. Realising Adam's somewhat impatient attitude, Gruff stopped sharply as a small wave washed up Adam's legs and soaked his jeans. Adam quickly stepped backwards as he looked down onto his now wet trouser legs.

'Great!' Adam snapped, brushing the water off his legs in some vain attempt to dry himself. 'You can't just say "change your life, Adam", then not tell me how I can actually...you know...change my life!' Adam bleated.

'Well let's see. Firstly, I didn't say change your life! I said, you need help to find happiness and meaning, to help change the direction of your life. Plus, I'm just a deck chair guy, who helps out at a beach bar, so what do I know about life, the universe and everything?' Gruff stated crossly.

'I'm confused. You said you'd help me!' Adam pleaded.

'I did, but I need to know that you're going listen, and trust me, because I'm going to tell you things and show you things that will challenge your current beliefs in what 'life' is all about. So, you've got to be able to 'see' what I'm going to show you. I'm not in the business of wasting my time and I'm certainly not tolerating some 'Karate Kid' attitude!' he said gruffly.

'Well, I know why they call you Gruff!' Adam snapped.

'Here's the thing. I'm not going to give you the answer to life. It's more like showing you a picture in a gallery and you can either see what I'm showing you or you won't' said Gruff, slightly more calmly. 'After that, it's up to you' he added.

'It's not going to be all weird and freaky religious stuff is it? No chanting and waving smoke around?' Adam asked.

'No, I'll just show you what I've learned, and you'll make up your own mind if it will fit with where you are right now... or not.' said Gruff, as he began to continue along the shoreline once more. 'What ya got to lose? Coz your life is a bit of a train wreck at the moment. Can't be any worse, can it?' he added.

'A train wreck! Thanks for that' Adam replied.

Just then, the conversation was interrupted by the noise of a small crowed gathering by the deck chairs stacked up against the sea wall. Adam could see what looked like a little old man and lady being hand cuffed by two policemen. They were being marched away along the sand towards the café car park.

'What's going on' Adam asked.

'It's ok Adam, I think the cops have caught the wallet thieves that have been operating on the beach. I gave them a tip-off earlier when I saw them casing the bar lounge area. We've been waiting for them to strike again so the police could catch them in a bit of a sting operation.' Gruff said proudly.

Adam could see they were the old couple (Doris and Ken) he had seen when he first arrived and had thought it was funny to imagine they were international crooks. 'Wow, that's weird...shocking' Adam said.

Adam then returned his thoughts to the lessons Gruff had been offering. He thought for a bit. 'Ok, let's do this!' Adam responded, offering his palm in the air (for a 'High Five'). Gruff raised an eyebrow and walked on through the lapping waves, leaving Adam hanging.

He quickly lowered his hand and skipped off behind Gruff's disappearing wet sand footprints, desperately trying to keep up.

'Do you have to walk so fast?' Adam shouted. Gruff ignored the request and marched on up the beach.

'The first thing you need to understand and take responsibility for, is that you are the reason you are where you are in life. It's that simple, because you, and only you are responsible for the choices you make', Gruff stated calmly.

'It's my fault. Really? How is it my fault? I didn't ask for this life?' replied Adam.

'Yes, you did! Look, you need to accept that you are in control of your own decisions, so you are responsible for the outcome of the decision you make! Until you accept that fact and take responsibility for it, you'll never move forward. It's your fault and only yours. No one else's, it's on you. Deal with it and then you can move on. Once you've done this, then you can become what you want to become. Simple, but tough to take.' said Gruff.

'You actually think I wanted to be this person? And it's my fault I hate my job and my girlfriend hates me? Wow! I'm not sure you're cut out for this guru teacher thing Gruff!' quipped Adam, taking a sip of his now slightly warm coke.

'I know it's hard to grasp. It is not an idea that sits well with everyone, but trust me, it's a fact. You are what you think you are, and you are a product of those thoughts! But think about it, the saving grace is that with this mindset, it also means you can change what you are by changing how you think. Thereby, changing your ultimate destination in life. Change your path Adam, to wherever you want to go.' said Gruff. 'But if this is too much for you, this ends here and now, and you can go on with your sad, dull, little flat battery of a life! It's up to you. Your call!' added Gruff.

'Ok, ok, let's say I change my thoughts, how does that change anything? I'm still here right now, with a badge with my name on it, in orange!' asked Adam.

Gruff laughed. 'True, but the key to this change in mindset is first knowing what you want to be and what makes you happy in life. Then you focus on seeing yourself doing whatever it is. If you can't see yourself doing it, no one else will. Then, change small things every day to move the needle in the right direction. Make it part of your life every day if you can. Then, trust me, you'll be amazed on how quickly things change when you just divert your attention and energy in the direction you want to go.'

'Right, I see...I think!' said Adam, nodding as he placed his thumb and index finger cupping his chin, trying to look thoughtful and enlightened.

'Let me give you an example. Take exercising. If you want to get stronger in the gym, would you pick up the heaviest weight any man has ever lifted straight away, or would you start light and progressively add small amounts of weight each week until you got strong enough to lift the heavy weights? It may take you years to lift what you wanted to lift, but you've achieved your goal through progressive overload and by getting stronger a small amount every day.'

Gruff stated, holding his oversized arm out, his salty cracked palms up to offer some kind of direction to the answer he was offering.

'I don't like the gym' said Adam. 'Full of steroid freaks!' he added.

'Ok, I think maybe my example is not the best for you to understand, so I need to show you the pictures first. I think I'll introduce you to some of my friends to help 'enlighten' you.' said Gruff, and with a slap on Adam's back, Gruff continued along the shore.

Learning outcomes:
- You are responsible for where you are today – it's on you!
- Find your 'why' in life.
- Find what would get you up early and keep you up late, for free.
- Find what gives your life meaning.
- Identify the things you get passionate about.
- Start at the beginning and go from there.
- One step at a time, every journey starts with a first step!
- Do a little bit of what you love every day and then slowly increase it.
- If you can imagine yourself doing anything what would it be.
- If you can't see yourself doing it no one else will.
- You get to choose.

*'If you think you can,
or you think you can't,
you're probably right.'*

Chapter Two
Sandcastles

The two men walked along the shoreline for a short while before stopping at a large, moat shaped excavation dug in the sand, which was the remnants of a sandcastle. Gruff stopped and motioned towards a father and son, kneeling in the wet sand a little further up the shoreline.

'Tell me what you see?' Gruff asked, pointing towards the sandcastle building team in front of them.

'Sand.' said Adam.

'Funny. Ok let's break it down a bit.' Gruff motioned in the direction of the small boy (of around 8 or 9 years old) and his father building a sandcastle by the shore, in the area of sand that was the border between the wet sand and dry, fluffy sand.

'Tell me what you see there?' asked Gruff again.

Adam put his hand slightly over his mouth and rested his chin in his palm (taking on his best thinker pose).

'Umm, well let's see. They're building a sandcastle. Father and son combo. Doing a reasonable job by the looks of it.' said Adam confidently.

The boy let out a shriek of annoyance as the water rushed over the sides of the sandcastle, and as it washed away it took a portion of the battlements with it. 'Aaarrrghh .... DAD!!' he shouted.

'Maybe not such a good job.' Adam nodded to himself.

The father and son team furiously dug faster and worked swiftly to repair the castle before the next wave came in. The joy of the repair was short lived as the next large wave crashed over the whole project, and with one swoosh of the returning water, the entire sandcastle was washed away leaving, only a slumped, wet heap and the semblance of the moat to show that it had even been there at all.

The boy sat back on his heels and his knees sank into the wet sand. 'Dad, it's gone. Uuurrghhh!' the boy moaned.

'It's ok Stephen, let's build another one a bit further up, but this time we'll build it twice as big.' The man put his palm out and the young boy slapped a high five and yelled 'Yeah, bigger!' They both laughed and plodded up the beach a bit and began to dig.

'So, what did you see, and more importantly, what could you learn from watching Stephen and his father?' Gruff asked.

'I'm not sure what you mean! It was just a father and his son having fun building sandcastles, wasn't it?' Adam asked.

'Ok let me tell you what we saw', Gruff said as he sat down next to Adam.

'Enlighten me.' Adam said, smartly.

'It may look to you like they are just "building a sandcastle" but look closer and you'll see that the father is teaching his son valuable lessons for life. He's not only teaching him how to build a sandcastle, that's just the mechanism for the lesson, it could be camps in the trees or tents from sheets in the garden. The important lesson is that no matter how hard you work, how much you care, or how important it is to you, nothing is forever. Sometimes, things in life will leave you, be destroyed, crushed, washed away. It's not in your control. You can care all you want, but these things are not forever. People, places, jobs, homes, and friends, like sand get washed away by the incoming tide of life. Eventually everything leaves, in some shape or form, from our lives. Sometimes they are replaced, and sometimes they are not. We often build things up just to knock them down ourselves. But often they are destroyed by forces outside our control.'

'The important thing is, we must recognise these aspects of our lives and not hold onto them, but let them go and move on. Take Stephen's beautifully constructed sandcastle for instance. The tide will always come in! "Time and tide wait for no man", as the saying goes. Stephen was disappointed at first but his father brushed him down and said, "Let's do it again!", because it was fun. He is teaching his son to understand that you must be aware of the things in life that are outside you control. But that doesn't mean you can't have fun on the way! Nothing lasts forever...nothing! But it's more than just a lesson in how nothing lasts forever, it is also teaching Stephen about teamwork and hard work, helping others even if you know the result will fail and your efforts are in vain. It's about enjoying the process, not the end result. Glorious failure is better than never trying in the first place'.

There was a short pause as Adam took it all in. 'Wow! I've never looked at it that way. I never built sandcastles with my Dad.' He pondered for a moment 'Lucky really, hey, coz they only get washed away.'

Gruff smiled. 'I thought you'd see it at that way!'

'Hey, Matt!' Gruff shouted.

The man with the boy turned around. 'Oh, hi Gruff!' he replied, with a wave.

'How's he doing?' Gruff asked glancing at the young boy kneeling in the sand.

The man walked over, leaving the young lad digging in the sand by himself.

'And how are you doing? You ok?' Gruff sounded sad and Adam wondered what was up.

'Yeah, not bad mate, thanks. I like to bring Stephen to the beach before we go up to the cemetery. He needs a bit of fun first.' He briefly stopped and looked up to the sky. 'Can't believe it's been two years already!' he sighed.

'Daaaaad!! Come on we've got to get the wall built. The tide's coming in!' the boy shouted.

'Gotta go, Gents, we'll catch up for beer sometime.' Matt shouted, as he ran back and jumped into the hole his son was digging. He picked the boy up and started to tickle him. The boy let out shrilled laughter

'Stop it Dad, stop it!' the boy giggled.

'Sure mate, looking forward to it!' he shouted back at Gruff.

'So, you see Adam' Gruff said quietly, 'not everything is forever. Life moves on'.

Adam sighed. 'That's so sad. Poor lad.' The two men continued along the sandy stretch of beach.

'Tough place to start,' said Gruff 'but there is someone else I think you'd like to meet' pointing towards a family group sat on a towel, behind a stripy rainbow coloured wind break.

Learning outcomes:
- Regardless of the actions and measures we take to protect what we have produced and created, some things will not last.
- This doesn't mean they're pointless or a waste of time, because they can also be great fun and great learning tasks.
- Take these tasks for what they are and be playful and have fun. When they are gone, just remember the joy they brought.
- Helping others is an easy way to find joy in any task.
- You've got to know when to let things go and move on.
- Life is tough, so go easy on yourself.

'It's not how hard you can hit, it's how hard can you get hit and keep moving forward'

Rocky V

Chapter Three

The Swimmer

The two men walked further along the shore, and soon enough, Gruff pointed out another person on the beach for Adam to observe.

'Ok, let's watch my friend Dave for a while, and see what you can learn.' said Gruff.

Adam mirrored Gruff's teacher like stance as the two men observed the slightly pale, and somewhat slim individual undertake what could only be described as a very odd version Thai Chi.

The pale tall man swirled his long, bony arm around his head, spread his fingers and interlocked them before pressing them downwards. He opened his hands, shook his arms, did a short jog on the spot and pushed his head, first to his left shoulder then to his right. He then twisted his head from left to right. Adam could hear the crack and shuddered at each 'crack'. He took a deep breath and ran at the breaking wave, with arms clasped above his head as the breaking wave engulfed the slim, pale figure. Adam looked on, expecting a triumphant projection from the swirling, white foam. Instead, he saw the slim pale frame of the swimmer's body thrown like a rejected bar of soap out of the crashing froth, back onto the shore. He coughed and spluttered a bit and, whilst grabbing his now failing shorts, wobbled to his feet and stood up before diving back into the torrent of white water. This dance of the flying bar of soap and failing trunks continued for a while, before a weary hand appeared above the back of waves and began to swim. Adam let out a gasp, 'Wow! I thought he was going to drown!'

'It's ok once you're in!' he shouted back to his unfazed, diminutive wife sat on the towel.

'Wow that was, err, surprising!' stated Adam.

'What was surprising about it?' Gruff asked.

'Well, for starters, why battle so hard and nearly drown to have a swim in the sea! Surely there are safer things to do? Or easier ways to get some exercise!' Adam suggested.

'Probably, but let's break it down again, so you can see that there is more to it than meets the eye. The struggle makes the success all the more satisfying, don't you think? This is man verses sea, and to get to the calmer water he has to run the gauntlet of the waves first. They are like the gate keepers to the kingdom. Dave has to battle with his fear, and the strength of the waves, to be rewarded with the calm water to swim in. Do you see?' Gruff asked.

'Not really, no.' said Adam. 'Seems like a lot of effort just for a swim!' he added.

As the teacher and student pondered the lesson, Dave stumbled out of the shore break, holding his shorts up with one hand and steadying himself with the other, as he briefly dropped to one knee before rising slowly, and trudged up the beach past the two on lookers.

'Hi Gruff, how's it going?' Dave asked with wet hair slapped across his forehead.

'Yeah good mate, really good. I see you're getting stronger in the water! When's the next trial?' Gruff asked.

'Oh, not for a few weeks yet. I'll be ready by then, 100%!' Dave replied.

'Adam, this is Dave. He's training for the lifeguard test,' Gruff said.

'Wow! Lifeguard, that's cool.' Adam stated.

'Gotta go Gruff, but we'll catch up for a morning swim sometime.' Dave said, walking past the two men towards his wife and jumping down on to the towel.

'Well done Honey, you are getting so good at getting through the waves now'! she said, wrapping another towel around his shivering shoulders.

'Sometimes in life you have to get comfortable with being uncomfortable.' Gruff quipped sharply.

'I'm not with you.' said Adam.

'Ok, so Dave's goal is to be a lifeguard, right?' Gruff said.

'Riiggghht' Adam replied, slightly unsure of where this was going.

'So, Dave has to get past the uncomfortable task of breaking through the waves to enable him to then start the task of learning to swim in the sea.' Gruff continued. 'He has to become "comfortable" with this first, otherwise he's never even getting started.' Gruff explained.

'Comfortable with being uncomfortable. Right!' Adam replied, still slightly unsure of the lesson.

'He knows it is going to be tough and he is accepting of that, so that he can get to the next stage. It's a bit like weightlifting to build muscle. It hurts, but you know that means it's working, so you accept the pain for the gain. Or trying for a PB running 5K. You know your lungs are going to be coming out of your chest, but it will be worth it for the PB and you'll be progressing, so the long-term goal is getting closer too. But you have to accept the pain and the struggle first, or you'll not be able to cope with it. Trust me Adam, nothing worth having is easy and moreover, most easy things aren't worth having.' Gruff said with a hard stare.

'Ok, so I get the "no pain, no gain" bit, but the guy looks so ridiculous struggling, coughing and spluttering. I mean, come on, everyone is watching him struggle.' Adam said 'Why would you put yourself through it?' Adam asked.

'Well, Dave nearly drowned last year, so he's been learning to swim, and because he was saved by a beach lifeguard, he wanted to train to be one, so he could help others if they got into trouble in the water. You see Adam, sometimes events in our life are there for a reason, and despite them being hard or traumatic they are there to provide us with lessons that in some cases spur us on to greater things. Just like Dave.'

'Six months ago, Dave still couldn't swim, but despite this shortfall in his ability, he never gave up on his dream. So, he focused on what he could control, and that was every day getting fitter, stronger and learning to swim and eventually he got to the point where he could get in the water and swim. Then he started pushing himself to get better and stronger, little step by little step. Now he's able to dive into the waves and battle the fear inside him, to make it to the calmer water beyond the waves and practice just swimming in the buoyant salty water. He doesn't care what you or anyone else thinks, he is focused on his goal and he will achieve it because he has a process and he's working through the process. Applying daily and weekly habits to improve his skills, getting better every day and therefore getting closer to his dream every day, regardless of how tough it is. Despite the fact that he has a family, job and life away from learning to swim, he fits it all in because it's important to him. It's important for everyone to do things that move the needle of their life and in Dave's case, actually improving the lives of others too. His dream is not a selfish, self-serving dream. His is in the service of others. The process is simple but never easy.' said Gruff, looking back at the small, happy family group on the sand.

'Brave guy,' said Adam.

'He's getting there one stroke at a time. Are you seeing the picture yet?' Gruff added.

'Yeah, I think so.' Adam replied as he looked down nervously at his sandy feet sinking into the wet sand, and not wanting to seem like he didn't understand the lesson.

'This is going to be harder than I thought!' laughed Gruff, as he once again slapped Adam on the back and marched off along the beach.

'I wish you'd stop doing that' Adam asked sharply.

'How would you want your life to be, Adam? If you could choose? It's a "Face down or Face up" type of question. Simply put, if you could choose, would you choose to have your face in the cold, wet sand or looking up at the sun, watching the waves and getting a tan? asked Gruff.

'Well, that's easy. Face up! Watching the waves... obviously!' Adam replied.

'So, turn over and face the sun. It's simple!' proclaimed Gruff, offering his large hands out to the sky.

'You've lost me' said Adam, slightly confused about where the conversation was going again.

'Ok, let's look at it this way. You get to choose your life, so choose carefully and make sure it is the one you want. You have accepted the face down in the cold, wet sand version for so long, you don't even know it, or that, more importantly, if you just turned over, the sun is shining and the sea is warm and inviting! You are the one who gets to decide which way up your life is, not your Mum, Dad, Girlfriend, your mates or your boss. You, and only you. You are responsible for where you are, what you are doing and how your life is right here and right now. It's on you...YOU!' Gruff explained, pointing into Adam's chest with a large finger.

'I'm still a bit unsure as to why it's my fault though?' Adam stated.

'Who asked your girlfriend out?' asked Gruff.

'Me!' replied Adam.

'Who applied for the job at the hardware store?' Gruff asked, looking knowingly at Adam

'Err, me.' Adam replied, sheepishly.

'Who chose the crap car you drive? The house you live in? Who decided to come to the beach today?' Gruff went on. 'You, you and oh...you!' he continued.

'Ok, I get the point. It's me, myself and I who's to blame,' Adam said, 'so how do I reverse these bad choices? he added.

'They are done, and in the past, but your next decision is up to you.' Replied Gruff. 'Look at this way. Say you were in prison and you had to make an escape plan? How detailed would it have to be to succeed? Very detailed, right? Down to last detail of timing and execution, right? Well you're not in prison so you don't need half the planning. You can just decide and make it happen.' Gruff explained, slightly frustrated.

'I love "Prison Break". Great box set, Adam proclaimed. 'Not sure about the tattoos though!' he added, with a sniff of a laugh.

'You've gotta start fighting for your future, Adam, because your happiness depends on it. You'll understand soon enough.' Said Gruff, walking on through the white foam as it seeped into the dark wet sand. Adam followed on a little nervously, wondering what the next 'lesson' would be.

Learning outcomes:
- It's going to be painful, accept it.
- Get comfortable with being uncomfortable.
- Your limitations are not reasons not to try.
- Failing is part of the process.
- Do the work.
- Focus on the small tasks to move toward to your goal.
- Good daily habits are the key.
- Don't be concerned with what others think.
- You decide your path.
- Help other people.
- Fight for your happiness.

*'Get comfortable
with being uncomfortable'*

Chapter Four
The Crab

The two men walked on along the shore continually, swaying as they walked, to avoid the washing waves as they pushed up the beach over their feet.

Gruff stopped abruptly and looked down at a small crab scuttling across the sand towards the water.

'Adam, look at the crab and tell me what we can learn from watching him make his journey to the sea?' he said.

'Ok, he's a crab, he is walking sideways on the sand and now he's stopped coz you've put your big foot in his way!' said Adam, slightly confused at the question.

'So, there is your problem, Adam, in nutshell. You see the world in a literal sense. As pre-set, with people just doing things for no particular reason, with no meaningful objective or sense of purpose. Just being, or surviving. You need to observe more, a bit like when you watch the people on the beach. I bet you make up names and give them strange reasons for being here, right?' Gruff laughed, somewhat sarcastically.

'Ok, what do you see?' asked Adam, trying to sound clever by flipping the question.

'Wow, answer a question with a question. Ok, now you're learning. Well, the crab is completely satisfied with his lot in life. He is a crab and knows what his sole purpose is. He knows his path and the meaning of life, which is to get to the sea, find a lady crab and make baby crabs. Plus, not get eaten on the way. He has a destination, the sea, and a path, the route across the sand, and we know he has a purpose. Plus, he knows what he is and who he is. So, in short, he has life sussed one hundred percent. But, my foot has given him a problem and he has to solve it, or he's not getting where he wants to go. More importantly, where he is destined to go. So, what does he do? He assesses the situation. Now, watch!' explains Gruff.

The two men watch as the crab tentatively taps a claw onto the side of Gruff's foot to assess the problem in front of him. Slowly he moves to one side, taps and then he moves and taps his claw again.

'You see what he's doing? He's working out the solution to the problem and adjusting his route to avoid the obstacle, whilst assessing the risk or danger from changing his route.' said Gruff.

'Ok, so what you're saying is that the crab had a route mapped out, but due to unforeseen circumstances, he has had to alter his original path to ensure he can continue on his journey to make little crabs with Mrs Crab? Right?' Adam replied.

'Right!' said Gruff.

As the two obstacles to the crab's journey stood discussing the lesson, the crab moved round Gruff's toes and off quickly into the safety of the shore break.

'There you go Mr Crab...go have your date night - Mrs Crab is expecting you!' Adam laughed.

'So, you get this lesson? You see that there is a path chosen, a route mapped and a destination waiting. But it's not always plain sailing. Right? You sometimes have to pivot to progress in life. But you must know your path first or you'll just drift with no destination. Or worse, end up on a path that you don't like.' Gruff said, knowing he was giving Adam the answer.

'Yup, I get it. What's next?' Adam asked, impatiently.

With Gruff's big hand on his shoulder once more, the two men carried on the journey along the shore.

Learning outcomes:
- There are lessons everywhere – just look for them.
- Before you start your journey, set out the route map.
- Just when you've got it sorted, someone puts their foot in the way to trip you up.
- If you encounter trouble or obstacles, alter the route or adjust the plan.
- Life is not linear – adjust / pivot.
- Never miss date night with Mrs Crab (she'll turn you into paste).

'Inch by inch...the inches we need

are all around us

in every break in the game'

Any Given Sunday

Chapter Five

The Golfer's Mindset

Gruff took Adam away from the sandy shore and up a path through the trees that boarded the beach. Adam had never seen this area of the seafront before.

'Jim!' Gruff called out to a man smartly dressed in a pink short-sleeved shirt, blue tailored shorts and a white baseball cap, carrying a set of golf clubs on his back. The man set the bag down with clink of steel as each club in turn settled in place.

'How ya doin', old man?' the golfer asked.

'Yeah good, we must catch up for round soon!' Gruff added.

'Absolutely, I need to get that money back off you!' he laughed. 'So, what are you doing off the beach? Run out of coffee to serve?' he laughed.

'I'm out for a walk with my new friend, Adam.' Gruff explained.

'Nice to meet you, Adam. Do you play?' asked the golfer with an outstretched arm, looking out down the fairway to the green.

'Not really, just a few games with mates back in the day, you know.' Adam replied, not wanting sound like he'd never played, which he hadn't unless you counted the crazy golf course in the local park.

'Do you mind if we walk a few holes with you as you play? Gruff asked.

'No, not at all' he replied, picking up his bag again and striding off to the teeing area.

'Adam, just observe what Jim does.' said Gruff, with a whisper.

Jim set his clubs down, picked up a small turf of grass, tossed it in the air and watched it fall to his left. He pulled the ball and a tee peg from his pocket and placed the ball on the tee peg, pushing the tee into the ground in one movement. He stood back from the ball, took the driver head cover off and dropped it to the side of the bag. With a gentle swoosh back and forth, he swung the club, each time looking down the fairway. Adam noticed Jim's gaze was soft but focused on the distance. It was like he was somehow in a meditative trance. Flowing back and forth, back and forth, looking and swinging rhythmically. He then stepped up beside the ball, hovered the club and swung the club, catching the ball perfectly, sending it soaring into the blue sky. It seemed to go on forever until landing on the soft, green fairway grass, bouncing a few times before rolling to a stop. Jim held his pose for a few seconds after the ball had landed and then with a 'tiger-esque twirl' the club dropped down to his side and was re-placed in the bag, head cover popped on and the bag was swept up and around Jim's shoulders once more, as he strode off.

'Shot!' shouted Gruff.

'Thanks, I'll take it!' Jim laughed.

Adam, Gruff and Jim walked on to where the ball had landed, and Adam watched as Jim repeated exactly the same routine. With his long iron and then again with a pitching wedge, sending the little white ball into the heart of the green. The two observers waited to the side of the green and watched Jim, now marking his ball and crouching down behind it. Then two practice strokes before sending the ball directly at the hole, it rolled up three inches short and Jim just casually tapped it in.

'Errghh, just a par!' he exclaimed in frustration.

Adam and Gruff followed Jim for a few holes, and Adam observed the identical routine on every shot. Shot, after shot, after shot. Grass, swish, look, swish, swing, twirl, club in the bag, and go again. Time after time. The zen-like routine.

The sound of the ball being dispatched time and again was broken by Gruff, 'Thanks Jim! Enjoy the rest of your practice round, and we'll definitely catch-up a round soon buddy'.

'No problem Gruff, I look forward to it.' he replied, walking off down the fairway to hit another perfectly struck shot.

'So, what did we just see?' asked Gruff

'A bloody good Golfer!' Adam replied.

'Yes, he is a great player, but what did you notice?' asked Gruff.

'Well, firstly, why is he not on the PGA tour?' Adam laughed.

'He is!' Gruff added sharply

'Oh well that's good then. Errr, well. He hits good shots and then hits...another? Adam asked.

'What can you take from what Jim does, into your life?' Gruff said, with a somewhat frustrated tone.

'Well, I could get another job and then play more golf, because I'd have more time?' Adam replied, again, slightly sarcastically.

'He knows the direction and the target for the ball. Then, he processes everything he can before executing the shot. Eat, sleep, repeat, for every shot. Routine, routine, routine... do you see?' Gruff asked.

'Yeah. I think so. That shirt though.... pink! Shocking!' Adam added.

'Ok, let's move on.' said Gruff, walking back down onto the beach. Adam followed, skipping down the gravel path and trying not to slip over.

The two men continued the walk along the shoreline before stopping by the group of surfers waxing their boards on the sand.

Learning outcomes:
- Focus.
- Dedication.
- Discipline.
- Be consistent and persistent.
- Routine, routine, routine.
- Learn your craft / skill.
- Eat, sleep, repeat.
- Enjoy the process.
- The results will take care of themselves.
- No harm in dressing the part!

*'See it,
believe it,
achieve it.'*

Napoleon Hill

Chapter Six

The Surfer

'What are they doing' Adam asked?

'Waxing!' Gruff replied.

'What's "waxing?"' asked Adam.

'Waxing is the time old tradition for surfers to prepare the deck of the board for the ride that's about to come! The wax, "sex wax", to be precise, is to allow their feet to grip the board and not slip as they ride the wave'. said Gruff.

'Sex wax?' Adam laughed. 'Really You're kidding, right?'

'No, not kidding.' Gruff pulled out a round 'puck' like product from his shorts pocket and offered it to Adam.

'Zog's Sex Wax' Adam read from the label. 'Who'd have thought...every day's a school day!' Adam chirped with surprise.

'That's the idea!' Gruff quipped, snatching the block of wax back and putting into his pocket again.

The two men watched as the small group of long-haired surfers sat on the sand, watching the waves and waxing, and watching some more.

Adam observed for a while and then asked, 'Why don't they just get in the water?'

Gruff laughed. 'Because they know that timing is everything.'

'Timing?' asked Adam. 'Surely the waves are there to be surfed, right?'

'No, just wait and see.' stated Gruff. 'The waves come in sets and each set has a wave frequency that needs to be understood, so they catch the right (best) wave of the set. They observe the breaking point and where the "tube" forms, so when they're in the water they've already visualised the ride before it's happened' Gruff explained.

'Dude!' one shouted. 'You coming? Surf's up man!' Gruff put his hand in the air. 'Naahhh, sorry Brad, got a friend with me. Maybe tomorrow? Weather looks good for the West Bay at the point.' Gruff replied apologetically.

'Cool see ya there early dude.' Brad replied, as he continued to wax his board.

Adam and Gruff watched as Brad picked up his now waxed board and ran with the leash slapping his ankle before throwing himself forward onto the board, as it skimmed across the shore break. Then, with an arched back, he swiftly paddled out, riding up the lips of the first few waves before dropping softly back down the far side of the wave, reaching the calmer waters beyond the breaking waves where he swivelled and sat upright, facing the beach. Adam was mesmerised by how smooth and effortless Brad had negotiated the initial breaking waves. Adam thought to himself 'he made it look so easy'.

Gruff slapped Adam's shoulder and laughed. 'Looks easy, hey? Trust me, it's not. It takes years of learning, failing, falling off and being knocked back before you can make it look effortless. Plus, he hasn't even attempted the hard bit yet!'

Adam then watched transfixed as Brad flicked his long hair off his brown, sun scorched face and began to paddle and with what seemed like one powerful pull, he popped his feet up and crouched, leaning forward slightly on the board with one foot forward, pressed down and cut back against the curling wave. A huge plume of water sprayed up from the back of the swooping board.

Again and again, rider and board swept across the face of the wave, long wet locks of hair flicked from side to side, with head turning, body swivelling, arms wide and knees bent. Each time spraying an arc of white water behind him like a peacock's plumage, showing off to the watching crowd on the beach. Then the wave fell away and Brad quickly flipped the small white surfboard to the top of the wave, and in one smooth motion dropped back to a lying position and paddled back out.

'Wow!' said Adam 'That was un'be'fuckin'lievable! Did you see that? Wow, that was so cool!' Adam shrieked.

Gruff just laughed. 'Look how he is in perfect tune with the rhythm of the waves. He knows when to paddle, when to ride and when the ride is over, each in perfect timing with the other. Seamless and effortless, as the full power of the ocean is channelled through his feet!'

Just then, the shout came from the other surfers 'BIG SET!' and like a group of demented penguins, all the surfers ran, leashes strapped to their ankles flapping between them and the board like over-sized rubber leg chains and jumped chest first onto their skimming boards to paddle out and catch the big wave.

The waves suddenly started to increase in size and noise level. Adam was aware now that a large crowd was gathering on the shoreline to watch the big wave riders attempt to catch the monsters that were starting to roll in.

'I've never seen them like this before,' noted Adam.

'Yeah, you have, you've just never looked before.' replied Gruff. 'Looking and seeing are different skills.' Gruff added.

'I don't know what you mean.' Adam had to raise his voice just to hear himself, with the now crashing roar of the huge roller colliding with the shoreline.

'You'll see!' said Gruff.

By this time the crowd had swelled to a few hundred people and the excitement was palpable, as the first surfers attempted to drop in on the monster waves rolling in. Each in turn, furiously paddling, pushing themselves up then jumping swiftly to try and stay on the board as it plummeted down the face of the wave, only to lose balance and helpless to the swift removal of the white stick beneath their feet, flipping them cartwheeling before disappearing into the soapy white foam of the crashing wave.

The crowd collectively held their breath until, like a leaping salmon, first the board, then the surfer emerged from the back of the wave. Hand in the air in a moment of defiance, and then saluting the crowds cheering on his safe return to the surface, unscathed.

The crowd gasped as the next brave soul attempted the impossible task.

'Look, that's Brad!' Adam shouted.

Gruff nodded and put a calming hand on Adam's shoulder.

Brad's tanned, slight, muscular frame was dwarfed by the huge wall of rolling water. The back of the board was picked up as Brad effortlessly jumped up to a crouching position and steadied himself, arms out, left foot forward, feet wide and knees bent. There was no bent knee kick turns this time, this was full out, high-speed survival at all costs, dare-devil, head down, downhill, big wave surfing. It appeared that Brad was virtually falling vertically down the face of the wave and seemed to defy gravity as he remained on the board. The tiny white stick seemed to flicker as the speed increased. Adam couldn't look away even though he was terrified that Brad would not complete the ride.

With the backdrop of the rising wall of mountainous ocean swell, and with a swift turn of speed at the bottom of the crashing wave, the tiny image of Brad and his white waxed board were engulfed in a wall of white foam.

'Is that it?' Adam shouted 'Did he make it?

No sooner had Adam asked the question, the crowd noise told him the answer. Whoops, whistles and shouts of 'Awesome!', as Brad's triumphant salute was seen emerging from the frothy foam.

'He fucking made it. Wow!' shouted Adam, just as Gruff slapped him on the back with a grin.

'Have faith my friend.' Gruff said, softly. 'Have faith.'

'All this excitement is making me thirsty.' exclaimed Gruff. 'Let's go get a coffee and you can tell me what you saw.

Adam and Gruff turned back along the shore to return to the café.

Adam sat back down at the bar and Gruff lifted the Bar hatch and proceed to make Adam a coffee from the gleaming silver Coffee machine in the middle of the bar.

'Black, white, sugar?' Gruff asked.

'What? Oh, white with one please.' Adam replied, still thinking about the surfers and the monster waves.

Gruff topped the coffee off with a shot of cold milk from the fridge and pushed the large, oversized mug across the bar to Adam. Adam took the cup and took a sip.

'Nice coffee, thanks!' Adam said, as he took another sip.

'Ok, so that was just a taster to show you the world is not always as you see it and sometimes you have to look before you will see, but when you look with different eyes, you see things differently.' said Gruff, pouring his own coffee and then taking a sip. 'I think I need some help to show you the path to a better life. Your life has stalled Adam and we need to get it back on track. You need to find out how, in any small way, we can put you on the right path. A path to a more fulfilling life, one that you can design and have control over in a good way, not like it is now. A pathetic excuse of an existence.' said Gruff, pointing a big, tanned, rough finger on Adam's chest.

'Ok old man. Easy!' Adam replied.

Gruff continued. 'So, I'm going to send you to see a couple of my friends that live and work around the seafront and the harbour. They will hopefully be able to enlighten you further and open the doors to the opportunities that you seem to be missing in life,' Gruff said thoughtfully, whilst fumbling around in draw below the spirit bottles and mixers.

'Yup, here it is!' Gruff shouted, as he pulled out a crumpled business card from the draw, pulled off what looked like blue-tac and presented to Adam.

Adam reluctantly took the somewhat scrappy bit of card and looked at both sides.

The card read 'John Atkins - Boat builder – No. 1, Dock Yard Lane.

'Ok?' said Adam, slightly confused 'I don't need a boat!'

'No, but you need to meet John. He'll help to put the next part of the puzzle together for you.' Gruff replied, as he swiftly took the coffee mug from Adam's hands, poured what was left down the stainless-steel sink and popped the cup up turned on the drainer. 'Don't worry, I'll wash it up later.

Now off you go. Oh, it's that way by the way!' he said, pointing towards the small side road, off the main seafront road.

Learning outcomes:

- When you change how you look at things. Things change how they look.
- Do things that scare you. It's good for you to know you're alive.
- Do things for fun and enjoyment.
- Failure is fundamental for success.
- If you don't fail, you don't know where your limits are.
- Playing is fundamental to success, as much as failure.
- Know what you can control and what you can't.
- Enjoy the success of others, and enjoy the ride

Daniel P Stimson

***'If you've never failed…
then you've never tried'***

Chapter Seven
The Yachtsman

Adam looked again at the card and read the address on the front of the old boat shed building sat on the dock side. He approached the large timber door slowly and was about to knock.

'Come in!' a voice from the other side of the door requested.

Adam pushed the door and poked his head in 'Hello?' he said.

'Gruff said you would be popping in for a chat. Come in, come in!'

The voice appeared to come from inside the hull of a boat tied against the pontoon, inside the boat shed.

'You must be Adam. I'm John.' the voice said, softly.

Adam felt calm and reassured by the man's voice, his soft tones somehow reminded him of his father's voice when he was a child having stories read to him. Just for a moment, Adam could see the flickering shadows of mobiles on his bedroom ceiling and could hear the faint noises of his father's car entering the drive, the headlights sweeping across the bedroom ceiling like a search light or a lighthouse. Adam was quickly snapped back to where he was.

'So, what do ya want to know young man?' the old man asked.

'Not sure really. Gruff has told me to be here to hear what you have to say!' replied Adam.

The old man appeared out from inside the hull of the boat with snowy white flecks on his face and in his hair.

'Here, catch this!' he said, throwing a cloth at Adam.

Adam caught it and placed it on the work bench beside him. The old man climbed down from the boat and brushed his head and chest down, sending white flakes of paint out into the air. He moved back as they floated down, like blossom from a cherry tree in autumn.

'Right then, do 'ya want a guided tour of the old girl?' John asked.

Adam smirked (that won't take long he thought). 'Ok!' he said politely.

'Well, she's a Hunter 24 and I've had the old girl for about 35 years. Picked her up from a guy needing some cash. Long story short, she needed some work doing, so I got a bit of bargain and I've been doing her up ready for my retirement. Then, I'm off on an adventure!' he said, proudly.

Adam looked a bit puzzled, looking at someone who should have retired a long time ago.

'Great, so how old are you?' Adam asked.

'Eighty-four...or is eighty-five? I forget. Who's counting?' The old man replied.

'Wow eighty-five! And when will she be ready?' Adam asked.

'Oh, not much to do now, and then I'll wait till spring comes around before setting sail. You can't rush these things. Gotta plan it right! You know the old saying "fail to prepare, prepare to fail", the old man said chirpily. 'Let me show you below decks.' he added.

Adam climbed over the railing and jumped down, bumping his head on the boom. 'Ouch!' he shouted.

'Mind your head on the boom!' the old man said, a second too late.

'Yeah, thanks!' Adam replied, tutting and rubbing his head.

Adam popped his head through the hatch and was met by what could only be described as a 'scrap heap'. The inside of the cabin was full of cogs, rods, cans of oil and rags. There was barely a place for Adam to put a foot, let alone venture inside and sit down.

'A bit of work to be done then?' Adam said still rubbing his bump.

'Yeah, always things to do. No rest for the wicked!' the old man replied.

Adam ventured back out and clambered down.

'When I bought her, she was in a terrible state. So I stripped the whole craft down to its nuts, bolts and cleats, so to speak. Then, rivet by rivet, bolt by bolt, put her back together again. It was slow going but each element restored was a step in right direction' the old sailor added.

'What are these?' Adam asked, pointing at a pile of maps and charts.

'The charts that will guide me on the journey. If you don't know the route, how do you get to where you're going? Every journey starts with a destination.' said the old man.

'How long have you been planning the trip?' Adam asked politely. Not wanting to sound uninterested.

'Let's see now. Had the old girl since 1979...' he said.

'Wait, you said you've had her 35 years?' Adam asked.

'Yes. What year is it now?' asked the old man looking slightly confused.

'2021' replied Adam.

'Really? Well, doesn't time fly!' the old man replied.

'So that's...' Adam started to count on his fingers, '20, 30, 40, err 42!' he informed the old man.

'Really!42? Wow!' he replied.

'So, let me get this right, you've been planning this trip and preparing this boat for 42 years, and you're still not ready to go, push off and set sail?!' said Adam, as he pushed another map to one side and watched it curl up like coiled spring of paper and roll off the desk. '42 years? Really?' Adam asked.

'Well young man, some things need to be planned and prepared for, the timing is key. It's all about timing' said the old man, proudly slapping the hull of the boat. 'Tea?' John asked.

'Err no, I'm fine thanks.' replied Adam.

'You can't rush these things. It's all about the detail. When she's ready, I'll be ready.' The old man stated, confidently.

Adam walks slowly around the old vessel, running his palm along the shiny blue hull 'This old sea dog isn't going to push off any time soon, but at 82 he's probably better off not going anyway.' Adam mumbled to himself.

'Sorry, I didn't catch that young man, what did you say?' The old sailor asked, cupping his hand to his ear.

'I said I need the loo, so probably best I get going!' replied Adam quickly.

'There is a toilet in the back, if you need to go.' the old man said stirring his tea slowly.

'How do you know Gruff anyway?' Adam asked.

'Well, long story short. I rent the boat yard off him and he helped me get the old girl up in the dry dock when I first started restoring her. He's been a real help to me over the years. Finding parts and lending a hand to rub the hull down or replacing the mast and stuff. Never too much trouble if I needed help.' John stopped momentarily and looked up. 'Always there when I needed him. Friends like Gruff are hard to come by, you listen to what he is telling you. Trust me, he's quite wise for someone so young.' John stated, proudly.

Adam laughed 'Young!' Gruff must be all of fifty-five, Adam thought.

'Well, I must be off John, thanks for the guided tour of the boat. She's a fine-looking craft and you've done a grand job in restoring her. Hopefully see you out on the water some time?' Adam said, as he reversed out of the boat shed.

'Ok young man, take care, and remember what I said - it's all about timing!' John laughed.

Adam slowly walked back to the beach. He could see Gruff talking to someone.

'Hi Adam' Gruff said.

'Well, that was strange!' Adam stated.

'Strange how?' asked Gruff.

'Well, I've obviously been to see John and his boat. He'll never put her to sea, will he?' Adam stated, confidently.

'No. John is a planner and a thinker. He has planned and thought about his trip for so long, the timing will never be right, the conditions will never be favourable, and he will always put an obstacle in the way of actually finishing the project. But in a way, that's his path. To restore the boat. But you get the lesson, right?' asked Gruff.

'Yup - fail to plan, plan to fail. Right?' Adam chirped.

'No!' replied Gruff.

'NO?!' Adam snapped back sharply, in surprise.

'No, the lesson was that you'll never be ready, so just fucking do it! If wait till you're ready, you'll never do it, you'll never start. I don't know....' Gruff said, shaking his head.

'I need you to go and see my friend Peter. He has a fishing boat down in the harbour. I've booked you a trip fishing for the day.' Gruff said, pointing towards the quayside. 'So, off you go, and have fun! You leave at 2pm sharp, don't be late.' Gruff added.

'Never been fishing before.' said Adam, nervously.

'Well, it's good to try new things and expand your horizons. Pete's boat is called New Adventures.' Gruff said, with a slightly sarcastic tone.

Learning outcomes:
- Know your purpose.
- Have a plan.
- Break it down into small chunks – one step at a time.
- Preparation is just that! It won't give you the answers for every eventuality you will encounter on the journey.
- If you wait till the conditions are 100% right, you'll never push off.
- Take the leap of faith.
- You'll never be ready.
- Take action.

'I love it when a plan comes together'
The A-Team

Chapter Eight
The Fisherman

Adam arrived at the quayside at 1.55pm and scanned the boats moored to the pontoon, there were hundreds of fishing boats.

'What was it called? New something...New Adventures.' Adam whispered to himself. 'New...arrgghh...there it is!' he said, somewhat relieved to have spotted it so quickly.

Adam approached the large, black and white fishing boat cautiously, it somehow reminded him of the boat out of the film, "Jaws". 'I think we're gonna need a bigger boat!' Adam said quietly, under his breath with a gulp.

'Hi there! Come aboard, you must be Adam? Gruff told me you'd be popping down and are up for a spot of fishing.' The voice came from a slim, striking looking man of about forty-five, and was bending over coiling rope on the deck.

'Yes, I'm Adam, but you know that already,' Adam said, nervously, 'I've never been fishing before....' Adam stopped, just as a loud American voice interrupted their greeting.

'Yo'll for hire?' Adam and Peter turned around to see a rather portly chap, in what can only be described as the worst pair of red chequered shorts they had ever seen, with a cigar in his mouth.

'No, not today.' Peter replied.

'I'll pay double!' the booming American voice responded.

This was Duke, an oil tycoon from Texas (a real bona fide Stetson-wearing oil baron). Duke holidayed here every year with his wife, Silvey and their two sons, Bret and Troy. He wasn't too keen on taking "No" as an answer for anything. He believed that everyone and everything had a price. Generally, a flash of the roll of bills usually did the trick. Right on cue, Duke removed the roll of cash from his 'sizable' shorts pocket and began to 'lick' his thumb and prize a note from the roll.

'What's it gonna take?' he asked. 50, 100...£150?' he smiled. 'My boys wanna go fishing and yours is the best boat in the harbour!' Peter turned around swiftly and responded somewhat aggrieved that this 'Oaf' assumed he could be bought.

'Sorry Sir, this gentleman has already paid for my boat today, and I don't do joint parties.' Peter explained.

'I'll tell you what, let's make it a round £500 and I'll repay your man here in full plus £100. What ya say, deal?' said the loud American.

Peter turned back to Adam, but before he could say anything Adam (feeling a bit embarrassed) said 'I don't mind sharing the boat, it's fine with me.'

'That's a deal then! Good call young man, we're gonna have a dandy day fishun'!" he boomed.

There was a short and slightly strained pause before Peter broke the silence with 'Ok. Let's go errrrr, fishun'', and for some unknown reason he slapped his thigh, like some sort of panto pirate.

Peter opened a box in the middle of the rear seats and started to throw bright orange life jackets at each member of the party.

'Chuck these on boys, it gets a bit choppy at the entrance to the harbour'.

The group pulled the orange life jackets over their heads, each in turn assisting the others with belt and the loop at the back.

'Take a seat!' Peter shouted, as he started up the noisy, diesel engine, which let off a 'bang' and a large puff of black smoke billowed out of the oily, steel exhaust positioned high above the wheelhouse roof. And they were off!

The boat forged its way out of the harbour mouth and out onto the open sea. The wake from the fishing boat spread out behind them, like the white tail of huge bird. The sky was clear blue, the breeze was warm and gentle, and there wasn't a cloud in the sky. A perfect day to be on the water.

'We'll head out west of the bay, to avoid the rip, and way anchor past the ledge.' Peter shouted.

'I don't know what that means!' said Adam 'but it sounds good to me!' He gave a short 'thumbs-up', grabbing the rail quickly as the boat flew to one side on the choppy waves. This was the first time Adam had ever been on a 'fishing' boat, and he wasn't sure he'd made the right decision to go.

'You'll get your legs in bit!' Peter nodded laughing.

Once again, Adam replied, 'I don't know what that means but...'

They were both interrupted by the sound of Bret throwing-up over the side of the boat. '

Hurr werrrrrugh....hurrr werrrrugh'!

'Better up than down!' Peter laughed.

Adam looked away as the young lad retched over the edge of the boat.

'WE'LL BE THERE IN ABOUT 10 MINS BOYS...HANG ON!' Peter turned the radio up to drown out the sound of, now, all three of the Americans throwing up over the side. The irony of the tune, 'Who's sorry now', blasting out was not lost on the group! Both Adam and Peter looked at each other and laughed.

Eventually, the boat slowed and Peter ran to the front and pulled sharply on a small metal handle to drop the anchor. Adam watched as the rusty metal links trundled quickly over the nose of the boat into the blue water. He ran quickly back along the gunnel walkway, jumped down into the middle of deck, opened a hatch, and kicked a large, red button. The engines quickly shuddered to a stop, leaving only the sound of the waves lapping against the hull.

'Right lads, let's fish!' The four faces looked back at him with somewhat uncertain smiles.

'How ya doing Adam? Gruff tells me you're a bit lost and need some help finding your path.' Peter said softly, not wanting the Americans to hear.

'Gruff's an interesting man, isn't he?' Peter said, before Adam could respond.

'Yeah "interesting" is one description, I suppose!' said Adam, sarcastically.

'He seems to know everything about me. More than I know myself!' Adam added.

'Yup, that's Gruff! He seems to know when people need a nudge in the right direction. He shows them the way, and then it's up to each person to see it for themselves. He helped me buy this boat with my Army Pension pay-out - best thing I ever did! So, tell me what you've learned so far, and I'll see if I can fill in the gaps.' Said Peter, with a knowing smile.

The two men sat silently for moment, both watching the seagulls dive into the waves and emerge with small, shiny fish, then attempting to fly off as another gull nose dives into them, resulting in a two-gull fight for the scrap.

'Ok, well, I've seen sandcastles being built and washed away. There was a swimmer who had to experience near death to crash through the waves and get to the flatter, calmer water to swim in. A crab who had to divert from his set path to reach the sea, an old surfer guy who was like meditating and surfing. Oh, there was an old yachtsman in the harbour where we've come from, who is planning for a long trip but he's been planning for years and never actually gone anywhere, and a golfer who did exactly the same thing before taking each shot' Adam recalled.

'No, you misunderstood. What did you learn? Not what or who did you see!' Peter asked.

'Oh, ok. Let's see, well, it all seems a bit confusing, but basically it looks like everyone sees their own situation from a different perspective, I think, but I don't see the connection between all the people I've met.' exclaimed Adam, somewhat frustrated.

Peter put his hand on Adam's shoulder. 'Let's see if I can make it clearer for you,' as he threw some more bait out into the water.

'There are dolphins and sharks out here in the ocean. They both live in the same environment, both feed on the fish and both continually search for the place they are meant to be. The dolphin has fun and plays in the waves, jumps at the bow of the ships and enjoys the ocean every day. The shark shifts angrily through the water searching for prey, attacking everything in its path. The dolphin is celebrated and enjoyed by all that are lucky enough to watch them play. The shark is feared and is sad and lonely, as it roams its domain.'

'Inside you there is a both a shark and a dolphin, Adam. Both are fighting for the right to exist in your ocean. An ocean of vast possibilities. Neither of them care about the other's desires, hopes or dreams. They will fight each other for the right to exist in the same ocean, but they are viewed very differently from the outside'.

'So, which one wins the fight?' Adam asked.

'The one you want to win the fight. The one you focus on. The one you feed the fish to. The shark is the fear inside you and the dolphin is the joy inside you.' Peter replied.

'OK, but I still don't see the connection between the dolphin and sandcastle?' said Adam.

'Look harder, Adam!' Peter responded.

'So, let me get this straight. The boy building the sandcastle was a lesson on perspective. You learn to build something that will always be destroyed, to understand losing and failing is part of learning and accepting that... nothing is for ever. See the task for what it is - something you can't control, so accept it. Right?' asked Adam.

'Right!' said Peter.

'And the swimmer was a lesson on knowing that the task is going to be hard, and it's meant to be so that succeeding is fulfilling and worthwhile! Because the pain is worth the prize. Right?'

'The crab?' Peter asked.

'Well, he had a route all planned out, but had to adjust to the change in the situation - Gruff's big foot - and he just managed it by assessing the problem and changing the route.' Adam said, confidently.

'Right again! You're getting there Adam. Keep going!' Peter cheered.

'And the golfer, what did he teach you?' asked Peter.

'That was a tough one at first, but now I know what Gruff was showing me. Focus on the routine each and every time, and then results take care of themselves - 'eat, sleep, repeat'. You just need to trust and commit to the process and be consistent.' stated Adam.

'Wow! Brilliant!' Peter added.

'Now, how about the Surfer?' Peter asked

'The surfer was experiencing the same wave as the swimmer, so he had gained knowledge and experience, but he was just having fun and seeing the beauty in the process regardless of how short lived it was. Oh, and they would celebrate catching a wave like it was the first time each time. They were all so happy for each other too, encouraging each other and cheering for each other. Plus, they experienced something that scared them', Adam added.

'Wow! Get you.' said Peter. 'Now, the old yachtsman in the harbour.'

'Well, I'm guessing he plans for every eventuality, but it's never quite right, so he never leaves the safety of the harbour. All the gear and no idea!'

'So what's the lesson?' Peter asked.

'If you just dream and don't act you'll never get where you want to go. You've just gotta take that leap of faith, and just do it.'

'Nice. You're starting to understand what Gruff is trying to teach you.

'Ooh wait, there were kayakers too. I'm not sure about the lessons from the kayakers. What was it, Pete?' asked Adam.

'Nothing, they were just kayakers! Not everything's a lesson, Adam!' he laughed.

'Now for the hard bit.' Peter paused and once again placed a strong hand on Adam's shoulder. 'What do you do now with what you've learnt?'

Adam thought for a while and said, 'I have absolutely no idea!' Both men laughed.

'Ok let's fish for a bit. I'm sure it will come to you.' Peter handed Adam some bait. He took it and threw it out into the choppy blue water. They watched as the bloody, fishy flesh slowly sank beneath the waves.

An hour or so passed, as the sun beat down on the bobbing boat. Not a word spoken as they watched the taut lines piercing the water. Adam took a swig of the bottled water. 'So this is fishing?' he said, sarcastically.

'Yeah, where else would you want to be?' replied Peter. No sooner as Adam opened his mouth, the line went tight and started to move away from the boat.

'I GOT A BITE! I GOT ONE!' he shouted. Peter jumped up and stood behind Adam. 'Ok, let him run. Now, reel it back. Let him run…reel it back…great, you're doing well.' Peter said, encouragingly. 'Keep reeling in and letting out just a bit, till he gets closer to the boat. He'll run out of steam in bit. Easy…easy…yesssssssss!' The fish broke the surface and Peter dived a net under it and pulled it onto the deck. 'Wow! A fish! I caught a bloody fish!!' Adam shouted.

'Yes, you did my friend! Yes, you did.' The three Americans watching in amazement continuously looking at each other and then back to fish flapping around on the deck.

'Bass,' said Peter, 'It's a nice bass'. They all laughed and clapped. Then Peter picked the fish up, pulled the hook and knocked its head on the side of the seat before popping it in the ice box in the middle of the deck. 'Let's get fishing boys. We're in bass country!'.

The group fished for a couple of hours and everyone caught a reasonable haul. Once the ice box was full, Peter stood all the rods up, pulled the anchor and with a huge plume of black smoke, started the big diesel engine. Before Adam had time to digest the events of their fishing trip, the boat chugged back between the large stone monoliths guarding the harbour's entrance like two large dogs.

Peter curled the ropes swiftly and dropped the hooped rings into the storage locker. Duke approached him with a large wedge of cash in his hand. 'Ever thought of expanding you little business?' Duke asked.

'I'm not sure what you mean.' Peter replied.

'Well, I can see what you have here, and I think if you were to borrow some money from the bank, buy another boat and employ a team to run the boat trips then you could, if you worked hard, built this business up until, say in about 10 years, you could have big fleet of boats and then you could franchise the model, float on the stock market, sell to a big international fishing corporation, and then you'd make enough money to retire like me and enjoy your free time!' Duke held his arms out and motioned them, as if showing Peter the kingdom he could have. 'Ok, I see what you mean. Just one problem.' Peter noted.

'If it's money for the first boat in the fleet, don't worry! I know a man!' Duke stated confidently, winking at Peter.

'No it's not the money bit, it's the other bit! You see, you say if I work hard for ten years I could retire and enjoy my spare time like you do.' 'Yup!' replied Duke.

'Well as far as I see it, you're on holiday with your boys here, where I live, and you relax by going fishing, which I do every day with my son, because I love fishing and spending time with my son. You want me to work hard, never see my family and risk everything for ten years to end up doing exactly what I already do in this beautiful place where I already live, with the people I love?' Peter pulled the cash from the tight grip of Duke's chubby little fingers. 'Naahhh, I'm good thanks.'

Adam jumped down from the back of the boat, turned and waved to Peter. 'Thanks Pete!'

'Anytime my friend, anytime.' Peter called back, mirroring the gesture.

Adam smiled to himself and did a little skip on the pontoon, grabbed the handles of the steps and jumped up the steps to the dock side.

Learning outcomes:
- Take action.
- Be prepared for some rough seas.
- Enjoy the journey.
- Know what you already have.
- Not every journey is yours to take.
- If you want to travel fast, travel alone. If you want to travel far, travel with people you love.
- Know what is important in life.
- Sometimes it's right there in front of you, but you need to look closer.

*'Life ain't all sunshine and rainbows,
it's a very mean and nasty place'*

Rocky Balboa

Chapter Nine

The Café

Adam could see Gruff leaning against the circular, wooden bar tables that wrapped around the poles supporting the tin roof of the beach shack bar. He had a knowing grin on his face, as he twisted a cloth inside a glass and placed it back on the shelf behind the bar.

'Sit down my friend, we have much to discuss.' Gruff said offering Adam a stool. 'Before you tell me all you've learnt, and I'm hoping it's a lot, I want to give the last piece of 'life's' puzzle,' he added, as he poured a glass of ice-cold beer and pushed it towards Adam.

'I want to tell you a story, or more a parable, about how time is precious and how your life should be organised. I'm not sure where I heard this, but it sums up your last lesson perfectly,' Gruff continued.

Gruff pulled a tray from under the bar and Adam could see a jar, some stones, pebbles and some sand. Gruff held the jar up in front of Adam, 'Is the jar full?' Gruff asked.

'No!' said Adam.

Gruff took the rocks and placed them in the jar and filled the jar to the top.

'Is the jar full?' he asked.

'Yup.' replied Adam.

Gruff then took the small pebbles and poured them into the jar and shook it until they fitted around the spaces left by the large stones.

'Is the jar full now?' he asked again.

'Yes, I guess it is now.' Adam replied.

Gruff then grabbed some sand in his hands and carefully poured it into the jar. It fitted into all the spaces left until the jar was full.

'Well, now is it full?' Gruff asked.

'Ha ha,' said Adam 'yes, now it's full. But what's the point?' he asked.

'You'll see.' laughed Gruff, who now took Adam's beer from him and proceeded to pour the beer into the jar.

'Now it's full Adam! Life is short and time is precious so you must organise your life in the right order of importance. The jar is your life and the space is the time afforded to you in life. The large stones are the important things in life, like love, family, friends, health and happiness. The pebbles are the other things that help to make our lives happy, like your job, home and the things you enjoy. The sand represents everything else that takes up time or wastes time, such as watching TV, social media or time worrying about unimportant things.' Gruff said, holding the jar up to Adam.

Gruff then emptied the jar out and poured the sand in first, followed by the pebbles and lastly, only 2 of the 6 big stones fit in, and only just!

'Ok that's great, but what does the beer represent?' asked Adam.

'Well, it doesn't matter how you organise your life, there is always room for a beer with a mate!' Gruff added with a smile. 'But,' said Gruff 'and this is an important but, if you put the sand in first, then the pebbles, the large stones won't fit in, and your life will be out of balance and a waste of time, because you will be focusing on the wrong things. Unfortunately, most people get the order all wrong and spend most of their time concentrating on the 'unimportant' things in life. Don't be most people Adam, time is so precious. Big stones first, right?' he added.

Adam nodded confidently, took a big gulp of the beer and with arms open wide said, 'Ok, I think I've got it. But I'm never going fishing again, it's way too rough and lumpy out there!' he laughed.

'Well go on then, give it to me straight and don't spare the horses' asked Gruff.

Adam took a deep breath, sipped some more beer, and began:

'I've got to know where I'm going before I set sail.

I must first take responsibility for where I am before I start.

I must be prepared for tough times but keep on going through the storm.

It's meant to be tough, otherwise it's not worth the effort (no pain no gain).

The journey is always better if it's enjoyed and shared with someone you love.

Plan and prepare, but at some point you have to push of and take the leap of faith.

Failing is an opportunity for learning, but it's only really a failure if you quit.

Change small things to gain the big thing. Focus on good habits so you don't get overwhelmed with the size of the task as a whole.

Clear focus, consistency and routine are key

Help others along the way and be kind.

Be your own person and remove negative energies from your focus.

Don't care about what other people think.

Show gratitude for all the positives things you have already.

If you can see it, you can achieve it, you just gotta want it bad enough!

Be the captain of your own ship.

Life is short, so put time and effort into the important things first, like love, family and health.'

'How's that for starters. Did I miss anything?' enquired Adam.

'Only a couple of things. Don't forget to enjoy the ride, go have a beer with your mates and, most importantly, HAVE SOME FUCKING FUN!' both men said together and laughed.

'Well done young man, you got there in the end and you have pretty much understood the lessons. I think you're ready for moving forward, but remember, you don't have to change where you are to change how you see yourself. Look around and take it all in, coz it's beautiful. Walk tall, be confident, take ownership of your life, follow your dreams, know what the end looks like and you will be just fine my boy. Most importantly, it's on you if you make it or not, you can't blame anyone else for where you end up.' Gruff said with a knowing smile. 'But not bad my friend, not bad at all! So, what now Adam? What are you going to do with the lessons you've learnt?' asked Gruff.

'Well first I will dig out my old camera, take some pictures and then...see what happens.' Adam replied, with a knowing smile.

'I wish you all the best young man and I'll look forward to you coming down here and snapping away at this old dog out in the surf. I might even commission you to take some pictures for my café, the place could do with some artwork.' Gruff laughed.

'I've got one last question though.' Adam said

'What's that?' asked Gruff

'Why the hell do they call you Gruff?' asked Adam

'Well, I suppose you deserve an answer. Ok, long story short. It's a surfer thing. My real name is George. George O'Donnell.' Gruff tilted his head and raised an eyebrow. So, my full nickname down here on the beach is Gruff Old Dog! To match my initials G.O.D. But most people just call me Gruff! It suits my voice too.' he laughed.

Adam chuckled, 'your initials are G.O.D. Wow, your parents had a sense of humour! Not too much weight on your shoulders with that one'.

'Well, we all have our crosses to bear in life.' Gruff added.

'Thanks, Gruff, you have opened my eyes to what I could be doing and most importantly, what I should be doing if I want to be happy and live 'my life' and not just 'a life', so thanks.' said Adam, holding out a hand.

'My pleasure, young man.' he replied, shaking Adam's hand firmly with a soft smile.

Adam walked away from the bar as the sun was setting behind him, he took a long look back and could hear Gruff talking to a young man sat at the bar. 'What's your story young man? Why are you here at the beach?' Adam laughed continued back to his car and drove home.

The next morning Adam rose early, with an excited apprehension for the day that lay ahead. He pulled his jeans on and after tipping the sand out, he pushed his feet into his trainers and with a quick sniff of his T-shirt (a nod of approval), he pulled it on and hurried out of the door. He stopped for a second and went back in, opened the bottom drawer of the hallway cupboard and pulled out his old college Nikon SLR camera. He took a couple of quick snaps of his feet, to check it still worked, then rushed back out and jumped in his car.

Arriving at the beachside car park, he was so excited about discussing with Gruff the plan he had made during his restless night. He pulled his car into one of the free spots, the engine had barely stopped as he grabbed the camera off the passenger seat and jumped out. He didn't even lock the door or stop to get a parking ticket - some things are more important, he thought to himself. As he approached the beachside railings, he quickly noticed the hard standing where yesterday he had sat with Gruff at the beach bar. A little confused, he thought he was in the wrong place. But no, this was the place, where the bar was yesterday. He stopped a skateboarder and asked, 'Where's the Beach Bar?'

'What Beach Bar mate?' the skater replied before pushing off and skating away.

'The beach bar, that was right…here. Excuse me!' he said to an elderly gentleman, leaning against the railings 'There was a beach bar here yesterday!' Adam exclaimed

The old man looked at the hard standing, then back at Adam.

'No, there's not been a beach bar here since 1987 son. It was destroyed in the big storm. George's old place' he said, before walking on, pulling the lead of his small, yapping pug.

Adam slowly walked back to his car, a little confused. He heard some shouting from the water. Four surfers were paddling out through the shore break. Adam shielded the bright morning sun from his eyes to look closer. One of the surfers looked a bit like Gruff, but this guy was much older, maybe sixty-five, seventy. Adam looked again as the old surfer turned towards him, the board's nose rose above the breaking wave and then dropped over the white peak and disappeared into the trough behind.

'No,' Adam thought 'that can't be right.' Adam shook his head turned and walk slowly back to his car.

'This yours?' a voice shouted.

'Yes.' Adam replied looking up to see the parking attendant now stood in front of his car.

'It's your lucky day! My pen has run dry. Move it, or I'll put a ticket on it pronto' the attendant exclaimed.

'Yes, it is!' Adam replied, smiling 'It's my lucky day.' Adam sat back into the car seat and then, without thinking, pulled the camera up to his eyes, turned towards the ocean, twisted the focus and zoomed into the four surfers paddling out through the shore break and snapped away at the seal like group kick turning and twisting on the crest of each wave. As he zoomed in to capture the old surfer kick turning across the breaking wave, he could see the old guy's face and was certain that as he took the picture, there was a nod, wink and a smile.

Adam sat back, started the engine and thought to himself, 'Stones in jar Adam, stones in jar. Let's get this journey started!'

The End.

Section 6

Lessons Learnt

Learning outcomes:
- Be the captain of your own boat.
- Enjoy the calm, sunny days, but prepare for rough seas if they come.
- The journey is better with someone you love, so you can share the experience.
- Don't just drift through life.
- Be mindful of what you are moving away from.
- Sometimes everything you need or want is actually right under your feet and not on a distant shore.
- When you know your direction, you will not be limited by weather conditions, storms or distance.
- You have everything you need to:
  - Have fun
  - Find joy
  - Have excitement
  - Provide for your needs
  - Help others
  - Reflect and show gratitude
  - Go in any direction that the wind takes you
  - Drive against or through the storm. Or....

- Drop anchor and stay exactly where you are
  - You'll never know how far you can go until you push yourself to limit of your capabilities.
  - I'll say it again….'If you've never failed then you've never really tried'.
  - **Just start…and see what happens!**

Section 7

Applying The Principles

So, the story, as you've probably worked out, is a series of short lessons based on some well-trodden paths and processes, which I told you weren't brain surgery or rocket science. They are, however, straightforward and practical, if used correctly and with a commitment mindset.

I purposefully didn't give the story a traditional happy ending, because the truth is the ending as such is up to Adam (or you) to decide. I'm sure you are asking 'Will he start a photography business? Will he leave his girlfriend? Will he ever pick up his Mum's click and collect shopping order?!' Who knows? Maybe that's my next book!

The real question is how do you apply the blueprint? Well that is, I repeat, ultimately up to you. You can take all of them in turn, or one or two, and apply them as you see fit, to meet your own end goal. It's not a one size fits all system, it's more like 'everyone has one size', so you just need to make it fit yours.

Mindset is everything! As the saying goes, 'If you think you can, or you think you can't, you're probably right'! This statement gives absolute clarity in understanding the power of your own mind. You have the power within you to do anything, (especially if someone else has done it before). You've just got to want it bad enough.

The basic toolkit is as follows:
- Start at the end.
- Visualise the final outcome in explicit detail.
- Take your attention from the 'whole' and place it on the first steps.
- Break it down into smaller chunks (one rock at a time).
- Create good habits each and every day.
- Move each day in the direction you desire.
- Be relentless, consistent and persistent.
- Planning is great but action is essential.
- Keep an open mind and learn on the way.
- Take the leap of faith.
- Celebrate all the small wins.
- Be grateful for what you currently have.
- You take your baggage with you, so make sure you can carry it.
- The journey is better with a companion.
- Keep your head up so you don't miss the scenery along the way.

Later in the book I set out my 14 rules for success. However, the above 'toolkit' is a basic list of essential steps to make the change in mindset.

IMPORTANT SIDE NOTE:

Procrastination is the killer of all dreams! 'Shoulda, coulda, woulda' doesn't wash when it comes to achieving your goals. Action is the key to success and action will get you moving forward. Like Rocky says, 'Keep moving forward.'

But to move forward you must start, and taking action is the only way for this to happen.

I should've done this, I could've done that, it would've worked if?...Sorry, but no one fucking cares, and that's the truth. People will react to positive, proactive movement (Newtons Law: every action has an opposite and equal reaction) - it's how nature works. Motion starts a reaction that leads to direction, that leads to things starting to happen and opportunities opening up. So just start. You'll work it out on the way.

Further side note: Actually changing 'who' you are is pretty much impossible! We are who we are. However, you can change all the elements that make up what others see as 'you'. Habits, health, fitness, outlook, perspective, academic knowledge and our own actions towards others.

Without question these are things you can change, and they will have a positive effect on your life and the people you love. Plus, in doing so you alter the direction of your life's journey and this may lead to new adventures you have never even considered possible before.

The cliché phrase is 'a better version of yourself'. It is still you at the end of the day, just a wiser, healthier, more energised, happier you. The core of you as a person will not change and any person or book that professes to suggest this can be the case is a fake. We are who we are, this book is about changing what I like to call your 'Fabric Response'. The external factors that put you in a better place, but at the centre and in the mirror it's still you!

Let me explain this a bit further. Your fabric response is the way you respond to external factors in life, and everyone has the capacity to change their response, because it's a learnt behaviour. An example of this is where two different people encounter the same situation but their responses may be very different. Take sky diving for example. Some people love it and do it for their job, others are scared stiff of jumping out of a plane. Same situation, very different response. However, over time the individual who is scared could, through exposure and training, learn to enjoy it. It's not the situation that defines you but your reaction to the situation, and that my friend is in your gift and under your control.

Section 8

How To Start

First you have got to find the time, and that bit is the easy bit.

'WHAT?!' I hear you cry. Yes, the very easy bit in fact.

SIMPLE TIPS ON FINDING MORE TIME IN YOUR DAY:

1. Stop endlessly scrolling Facebook and Instagram. Simple! Just look at the data information of your screen time and you'll see hours of wasted time.
2. Get up earlier. If you normally you rise at 7am, now rise at 6am instead, and you'll have an hour free to do whatever you want.
3. Stop binging box sets / Netflix series – they are brain killers creating negative emotions and furthering addictive traits. More time saved! Hours and hours, even days could be saved. I could write another book on how damaging tv binging is for you when it comes to wasting time.
4. Plan your day better – a simple plan of tasks will provide you with a better understanding of how your day is laid out and how to group tasks to reduce wasted time in between.

The above examples are just 4 simple ways to create the time to do the things you now need to do to move in the direction of changing to the new version of you.

Yeah, I know I'm a total bastard, and now your life is so dull and mundane you want to just crawl back into your warm bed and cry! But guess what? This mindset is exactly why you never get anywhere in life!

So, you've bucked up and come off 'Wastebook', thrown 'Breaking Sad' series 28 box set in the bin and grabbed some paper and a pen (or pencil, either writing implement is acceptable and both available from all good stationary retailers). Once you've been brave enough to do this you can now address the other burning issue. Where to start.

First, start by making the plan of how you are going use the hours you now have free in your day. We'll get the details of designing your day better a bit later. But for now, just celebrate the fact that you are now free from Wastebook and box set misery.

Side note: Rule 12 - celebrate small wins. Yay!

WHERE TO START

Well done! Now you have loads of time on your hands to plan the route to your goal. If you don't know what this is, (see Rule 1. Find your passion) you are not alone. Trust me, there are millions of people who just don't know what would give their lives meaning, but they know that what they have or where they are in life isn't it. You need to be clear on this before you start or there will be trouble ahead.

If, however, you do know then well done you, as you are ahead of the game already. 'Begin with the end in mind' - this is one of the great principles of my system and has been utilised by the great stoic philosophers for centuries.

Let's break that down a bit. Starting at the end is a key fundamental of any journey. Why? Because the vision of the end result gives the neocortex area of your brain, the part which is responsible for imagination, the clear picture of the desired outcome. This is key for your mind to then understand the reason for the task – habits, pain, sweat and tears that you are going to experience. By visualising the end goal, you will be setting your mind off in the right direct from the start. Please do not underestimate the power of visualisation as a weapon to achieving your goal. Your brain is far more powerful than you give it credit for, so let it do its thing.

Side note: I'm not talking about visualising the end of your life (though some advocate this to scare you into action, but that's a different book all together!). I'm talking about all those small journeys you can take to change where you are in life.

Also, when I say 'visualise', I mean in fine detail, not just non-descriptive, pointless statements that have no basis in reality and more importantly cannot be achieved, or at least they are so vague that a ½% improvement means you've succeeded. For example:

I WANT TO BE THINNER

I WANT TO BE FITTER

I WANT TO BE STRONGER

I WANT A BETTER JOB

These non-descript statements mean nothing!

More importantly, they actually harm your likelihood of success, because they don't help you to create a meaningful image of the outcome, and because they are so vague they don't allow your mind to rationalise them as realistic achievements that need attention. You need to drill down

SINK OR SWIM

into the detail. Be specific, be creative with the imagery, get microscopically specific with the minutia of the task in hand.

Let's take going on holiday for example. You always know where you're going (the resort or hotel), how you're getting there (the flight or train etc), when the flight leaves, when it lands and how you will transfer to the hotel. You never leave these to chance, because it's too important to know if the hotel is near a nice beach or in a nice part of the city, if the facilities match your needs for swimming or going out in the evenings, or if the local restaurants are good. So why treat your own 'life' journey any differently. The holiday in Corfu is just 2 weeks (and you can always go somewhere else next year), your life is forever! Why take the chance on not knowing the destination? Or at least understanding the path you set out on. Why leave these important things to chance?

If you do nothing else, or take only one thing from this book, it should be to start by visualising the finish line. Moreover, visualize you crossing that finish line. See it in your mind then write it down in fine detail and refer to it regularly. I can't stress this enough. If you can see it first, you have half a chance of reaching it. Without it, you have zero chance. I'll take 50% over zero every time.

This principle works whether you are seeking business success, fitness, overcoming addiction, improving relationships and everything in between. Trust me, every person that sets out to achieve anything in life, and every book ever written on the subject, has this visualisation principle at its centre. Therefore, you must too.

Back to the story's lessons

In the story section we see our 'hero' Adam, seeing everyone else experiencing life whilst he sits on the side lines, moaning about his flat battery of a life. He is reluctant to dip his toe into the water, he sees people failing, embarrassing themselves and struggling generally. He uses their situation as a reason not to even try in the first place, he uses their responses as support for his own fear of failure. He sees the diamond glint of the mainland, metaphorically speaking, as being out of reach to people like him. His perspective on life is narrow, he can't see the bigger picture, he fails to see (excuse the pun) the importance of failure as a mechanism to success or as tool for learning. So, he doesn't even try, he just moans about his own sad, stressful life and tries to relieve the pain and the stress by taking a day off now and then. This is a short-term solution for a long-term problem.

Adam's basic, closed mindset is 'blinkered and fearful'. He has a limited belief in his own ability. Even to the point that he stops himself from even having some fun, just in case (in his eyes) he fails or makes a fool of himself in the process. What would his Mum say, or his girlfriend, his boss or even complete strangers? These excuses and reasons for not trying, arise in people's minds all the time and are barriers to moving on up in life. They are, by definition, 'limited' in their belief in their own abilities. Adam is happy (relatively speaking) to be a spectator in his own life. He just wants to sit on the side lines and watch everyone else have fun, just as long as he doesn't put himself in a vulnerable position. Does this sound familiar?

Adam is a normal 'flawed' individual, just like you and me. We all have fears and we all put our (misguided) belief in the outcome as the reason we don't even start something just in case we fail. Fear of 'what would people say' is one of the biggest killers of success. But there is hope, because the fear of the perceived negative outcome lives in your own mind. It sits in the future, it's not real. The future is not set yet and therefore we could, if we so wished, just re-frame the outcome with a positive result. The decisions we make control our destiny. Don't let fear guide your decision making.

Apart from the fact that fear is not real, more often than not, if we try, we will succeed (even if takes a few goes) and our initial fear of a negative outcome never actually manifests itself. Moreover, actually doing the trying bit and failing bit, that's the fun part...isn't it?

How boring would life be if you could do everything you tried first time?! No sense of achievement, no pleasure of overcoming the difficulty of task, no reward for your effort. No joy in winning! How sad would that life be? You will, ultimately, only find how far you can go if you push yourself to the limits and I'm only suggesting you try something that makes your life better, not something that might end it.

Contrary to popular thinking and perception, I'm not a reckless person, far from it. I like to plan and analyse things. I don't take foolish risks. I want to know the plan first, then I act. So, I'm not advocating trying things that are dangerous with outcomes could be the end of me! There are certain crazy people that will do these things in life, I'm not one of them. Like sky diving without a parachute, or swimming with great white sharks. Noooooo...don't do those things! I'm talking about those journeys in life that move the needle. Your personal needle that moves you on in life. Those amazing things that make you that better version of you we spoke of and allow you to grow. The dreams that are worth chasing. Health, fitness, that business you dream of running, love, relationships. These things are worth chasing. The ones that make getting up on a Monday exciting, meaningful and purposeful.

One of the key lessons from the story is that preparation is important but you will never be 100% ready, and you will have to take that leap of faith and learn some lessons on the way. If you wait till you're 100% ready with everything you need, you'll never start! There will always be that 'one thing' that stops you. So just jump! You'll work it out on the way down. Or, you'll hit the ground with a thump, and if you do, dust yourself off, climb back up and jump off again, and again, and again, until you fly.

Everything that has ever been achieved in this world, created or invented, started out as a dream. A spark of an idea, which was quickly followed by long periods of failure, re thinking, going again, failing again, re modelling and failing again, and again until it worked, or they succeeded. Nothing worth having comes easy...nothing!

Anything you can imagine is achievable. Period. Don't let anyone tell you different. If someone else has done it then you can too. More often than not when something deemed 'impossible' is then achieved, it is reduced to the status of just 'difficult'. Then it's just about how much you want it. It's on you! Because it's not impossible anymore. So back yourself and go get it.

Having a 'Growth Mindset' is key to achieving anything. What I mean by this is you must be open to ideas, to learning and gaining experience in all aspects of life, not just the area you want to progress in. A growth mindset puts dreams into motion, with the premise that nothing is unachievable and therefore you're only limited by your own imagination. Far too often, people are limited by their own beliefs and value structure. You must abandon this mindset and be open to expanding your thought process to 'nothing is impossible'... nothing.

Adam obviously gets there in the end, but needed a little push along the way, and eventually his eyes opened to the process and blueprint that Gruff showed him. This is where my book helps. It's the push you need, but you need to be clear in which direction I'm pushing you. This is very different to depending on someone else for motivation.

I have a strong opinion on the classic notion of motivation. It is, in my opinion, innately internal and not, as some lead you to believe, external. In the next section I'll explain what I mean by this. But know this much, you must understand the difference between internal motivators and external ones if you want the change to be sustainable, meaningful and worth the sweat and tears.

Section 9

Motivation

This is one of the most asked questions or excuses I get thrown at me. 'I'm not motivated,' or 'how do you stay motivated?'. Well, the thing about motivation is, as we are led to believe, that you get it from somewhere 'external' like a magic pill or potion, or worse, that it is something you need to pay for.

Well I'm here to tell you that is all bullshit - 100% total crap! And here's why.

(Side note: I've not got an issue with personal trainers… just what people use them for!)

Motivation is internal, not external. Let me explain:

- If you don't have it to start with, it's not your journey to take.
- If you need someone else to tell you need it, then you're wasting your time as it won't last.
- It has to be you. From the inside from your 'gut'.
- If you're not doing it for you then the results will be temporary.

I know it sounds harsh and there will be loads of you telling me I'm wrong, but in my 54 years (nearly 55 at the time of writing this book in 2021) the only sustainable changes I've made are driven from inside me, because I wanted them.

Not to say wanting things for my kids, or for my wife, or for my Mum and Dad is bad! Far from it. External drivers are powerful, but they aren't from your gut or from your dreams. They are because you love those individuals and want to please or help them. There is nothing wrong with that, but, and it's a big but, it's not from inside you!

Trust me, no child ever said 'I'm glad I never see my Dad because he's starting a new business and working all hours!' No truly loving spouse ever said 'I will love you more if you're thinner or have more muscles or earn more money.' These are false motivators. Don't use false motivators to underpin your beliefs in your dreams. Your family will support you if they can see it is actually your dream.

Now let's be clear, before you get all self-righteous on me, having support for your dream is very important, and your family and friends are going to be key to your success 100%. BUT THEY WILL NOT MOTIVATE YOU TO ACHIEVE YOUR GOAL! They support you, that's their job and their role in the process. To support you, but not to motivate. That's not their role, there is a difference.

You need to reframe the word 'MOTIVATION' and set it in its rightful place 'INSIDE YOU'. If it's not there naturally then it's not going to be there artificially. So, go find one that is there naturally. Find your 'WHY' (See Simon Sinek's book *'Finding Your Why'*).

How many stories have you heard of people who lost their way mid-life because they were following what their parents wanted for them. The classics are people becoming a doctor or a lawyer when all they wanted was to be a painter or a dancer. They might have lost many years on the wrong path, with the false notion that it was right that they should be doing it for someone else. Think about it, you must follow your dreams not the expectations of others. If you don't, you will be unfulfilled and searching until you do find your path, or until your final day.

A famous man once said the richest place on earth was the graveyard, because it was full of unfulfilled dreams. You don't want to have the ghost of your ambition sit on your death bed with a list of unfulfilled dreams.

So, what are false motivators and how do we spot them? Some false motivators are all those things that are 'things' and they live in the physical world or come from a place that other people can judge. They are the outcomes or by-products of the process, that we see as important for such things as validation, respect or recognition.

Or worse, they come from fear, greed and envy. These motivators are destructive, damaging and take you down in the end.

Trophies are all very nice to have, but shouldn't be the motivating factor. If they are your key driver then the satisfaction from results is going to be hollow and short lived. You must be driven by the true motivators.

False Motivators:
1. Money
2. Prestige
3. Trophies
4. Respect
5. Credibility
6. Acceptance
7. Validation
8. Greed
9. Envy / Jealousy

True motivators are the <u>reason</u> we want to achieve the goal, not the prize itself. They are found in your heart and your gut. They are nebulas and subjective, to a degree, but all are worthy causes.

True Motivators:
1. Love
2. Passion
3. Dreams
4. Joy
5. Happiness
6. Health

These motivators are from inside and will drive anyone onto success. They are sustainable and are the foundations of a fulfilled life. Think about it, which would you rather have on your head stone?

'THEY WERE RICH AND SUCCESSFUL WITH A WEALTH OF PRESTIGIOUS TROPHIES TO THEIR NAME'

or:

'THEY WERE PASSIONATE, MUCH LOVED AND LIVED A JOYFUL LIFE FOLLOWING THEIR DREAMS'

I know which I'd prefer!

True happiness and fulfilment come from following your dreams, not hoping people will notice what you've achieved.

The Harsh Truth: 'It's on you!'

This is the toughest lesson of all, in my opinion. 'It's on you'. You are where you are because YOU designed it. Your life that is, this way. No one else. You! I have a mantra for this aspect of life and a lot of people have questioned it and argued its validity. It goes like this:

'Of the things in life, that you can control, you will get what you deserve'.

Caveat: The mantra is purely focused on, and relating to, what you 'can control', not what life throws at you when you're not looking - like bereavement, health issues or sickness etc. However, having said that, our reaction to life's curve balls is still within our control, even if we didn't ask for a tumour, dyslexia or whatever life threw at us when our backs were turned.

Harsh, I know, but absolutely correct. It's all on you, so don't complain - do something about it! The real truth is that life is tough, so grow some and crack on. Life is something that happens to you whilst you are busy doing something else, so make sure the something else bit is something you love.

For me, the sense of achievement and what makes it all worthwhile, comes from the relentless pursuit and dedication to the process. Too many people want the end result but not the tough journey to get there. They want the prize without putting in the real hard, painful, dirty hard yards. You have to take responsibility for who you are and where you are. Then, and only then, can you move on to higher ground.

For example, take reasonability for the fact that you created this sugar monster of a body. If you really want a body for the beach next year, then put the work in during the winter to achieve the physique you desire. But you've got to be prepared to go through the pain barrier, sweat and tears, get up early, miss meals and do all the things that are required to achieve the body you want.

If you don't and you're not willing to put the hard yards in, then you probably didn't want it in the first place, or you didn't want it bad enough. The problem with most people (don't be 'most' people) is, they find every reason and excuse not to do it and blame everyone and everything for why they didn't get there. Definitely don't be that person!

Generally, I find the people who do carry through on their dreams are the ones that enjoy the process. The ones that like the puzzle of it all - the journey. They enjoy solving the problem and putting the pieces together to get across the line. They are usually relentless in the pursuit of their dreams. Whether it's body builders, athletes, leaders in business or entrepreneurs. They have a dream and they work relentlessly towards the realisation of that dream. Nothing will stop them and they don't care what you, or anyone else thinks of them. These are not ordinary people and, unfortunately, most of us mere mortal humans are just 'ordinary' people and are just not wired that way. If you were, you'd not be in the position you are now reading my book. Trust me, Elon Musk and Arnold Schwarzenegger are not reading my book.

As with all new things in life, this process and mindset change needs practice. You'll need time to fail and learn, but you must get obsessed with the process and the detail of the process to form the habits that will become routine and then innate aspects of your daily life. Please don't think this is easy, it is not. Obsessed, relentless individuals make it look easy because they are immersed in the detail of it all. You must be too.

A word of warning though. As we have already discussed, make sure you know 'your' path, the one path that makes you happy and is part of the fabric of your dream to give your life meaning. The worst thing for us 'mere mortals' would be to follow a path that is not yours to follow. Without fear of contradiction, you'll end up in a worse position than when you started. Far too many people follow a dream that is something they think they should do, or are compelled to by a misplaced loyalty to a mentor, teacher, parent or child.

Following someone else's dream in the end will be more painful than failing at your own dream, because, once you realise you've wasted your life following this false prize, you will be further away from the real one. You're far better off continually failing following your own path than one that is not yours to follow.

There are two very good reasons not to climb someone else's mountain. Firstly, once at the top it's a long way down. Secondly, once you take the tough decision to climb down, once you are at the bottom again you've got another mountain to climb. That's a real motivational killer! Trust me on that one.

So here we are, finally, at the list of 14 rules. If you have got this far you'll already know most of them and understand how to apply them. But I'll break them down so you can see how each in its own right is vital to the process.

Section 10

My 14 Rules For Success

1. Find your passion
2. See the bigger picture
3. Visualise the end goal
4. Form small daily habits
5. Be comfortable being uncomfortable.
6. Find a way of including 'it' in your life
7. Design your day
8. Find likeminded people
9. Educate yourself on the way
10. Back yourself every time
11. Don't waste time
12. Celebrate small wins
13. Don't Fear 'fear'
14. Have some fucking fun

1. Find your passion

It's a cliché, but a good one. Finding your passion, or meaning in life, is the key to finding joy and fulfilment. So, what is it? It's the one thing that makes sense to you, the one thing that holds the key to your own personal happiness. But the big question is, if you don't know what it is, where do you start?

First, find your 'Why' (read Simon Sinek's book *'Finding Your Why'*). It's not easy but it's vital to moving forward in the right direction. Also, the process of finding it is not straightforward if there isn't anything obvious in your life that is your passion. Don't worry, you're not alone but the process to find it is worth it.

Make two lists. Start by making a list of all the things that you think makes you…you. Then, list things that you could do that would make you happy in connection to the first list. Things you would love to do if you were paid for doing it, better still, what would you happily do and not get paid to do it.

Put the two lists together and look for the commonalities, the connections. Once you have found them then you are halfway to knowing what it is and what it looks like. Achieving 'it' is only possible if you put in the work.

Mind mapping and cloud connecting on a white board is a really good way of contextualising the two lists. You can stand back and see the bigger picture of all the things in your life that makes you 'you' and makes you happy.

Word of warning though. Too many people go through this process then sit on it as if it's just going to happen all by itself. It won't, you've got to make it happen and do the work. You have to take action.

2. See the bigger picture – Perspective

The best way to find something that you are looking for is to start looking for it. Sounds simple I know but it is true. If you can't find it then re-frame what you look at. There's so much more to see than you think, if you look hard enough and wide enough. Open up your field of vision and see the wider perspective on the situation you find yourself in and see what is hidden behind the frame, hidden from view. Only when you can see the whole thing will you see the answer to the question. Perspective is everything when trying to understand or solve a problem. Too many people focus on a small point of the issue and miss the wider situation, so don't get blinkered, get your head up and look around. Also try moving your position to someone else's position, then you'll get the perspective from other people's view.

What do I mean by this? You need to see the outcome from both situations. What happens if I do start and what happens if I don't? the outcome will change as every decision is made, so you must know the action and opposite reaction to the decision. So, stand back and picture the future with the goal achieved. What does that look like? What does it look like without it? How does it affect the people around me? Positive or negative?

Healthy eating and understanding nutrition are good examples:

I want to lose weight so I need to make better choices around my nutrition. But that might cost more money and might be harder to carry through, because my kids eat pizza, chips, crisps and chocolate. But, if I take a step back and look at the bigger picture then if they all eat healthier too that would be good for them. Perhaps I can get the whole family to eat better which will make it easier to afford and has a net gain for my family's health generally.

By seeing the wider perspective on things, you will quickly get a sense of their effect on both your long and short term, and those around you. It will become abundantly clear if the pain is going to be worth it.

3. Visualise the end goal

You've found your passion, the one thing you want to do or achieve. Now you need to see yourself doing it or being it.

If you can't see you doing whatever 'it' is then no one else will either. Because the phrase 'act as if it already is' and the word 'yet' are two very powerful statements and ones you need to get to grips with.

Think about it for a minute. If you haven't achieved your dream but include the word 'yet' in the sentence, that means you are still in the game, still fighting, just not there yet. Add the power of visualisation into the equation and suddenly anything is possible.

As the saying goes, 'See it, believe it and then achieve it.' You won't achieve it unless you can truly see yourself doing it. Half the battle with any goal is this lesson, but it is a tough one to get over for most people. They want it, they think they need it, and even believe they deserve it, but find it really hard to visualise themselves actually doing it. Re-read the 'Surfer' chapter of the parable where the surfers sit and watch the waves, visualise themselves catching and riding the wave to its conclusion before even attempting to go into the water. The ultimate 'dry run'. They watch and learn and visualise how the wave is breaking - how that feels, smells and even how it sounds. Then, when they have the 'rhythm' of the wave they commit 100% to the process, because once in the water there is no going back - they are all in.

Side Note: The one missing element that is very, *very* important is how you start the process, and this is something that most people misunderstand, or worse, (ironically) ignore it. Because you **must** ignore (I said it was ironic), yes, ignore the end goal, or at least take your main focus off it and focus on the habits that move the needle. Let me say that again 'You **must** take you focus off the end goal! It's the habits that you change in your daily routine that will define the path to the prize. The final outcome (prize, goal, weight or position), will be a by-product of good 'daily' habits.

4. Form small daily habits

To make a big change manageable, you need to break it down into its smallest parts and thereby easier to manage. If you look at the whole mountain there is no way on earth you are moving that in one go. It's too big. But pick up a rock and move it, then another, then another, suddenly the mountain is moving bit by bit. The trick is committing to moving one rock at a time, not too many at once, then progress can be manageable, sustainable, achievable and importantly, measurable. Being relentless with the small things will make any task easy if you stick to the process for the duration. You'll find it far easier managing small elements daily than stressing on the whole task.

Dr Jorden Peterson says in his book '*12 Rules for Life: An Antidote to Chaos*', 'get your house in order first, then see what happens'. He gives an example of just tidying your room. Sounds simple, but the ripple effect could be huge, so just do it. If you want to change the world, start by changing your world first then go from there.

5. Be comfortable being uncomfortable

This is a really important aspect of the system and must be accepted. If you don't do the work and put yourself through the process with the clear understanding that it's going to be tough, you will fail. It's meant to be painful! You must, I repeat must accept that (note: in legal terms 'must' is non-negotiable term). Doing nothing is the easy path. But easy never gets it done and easy will never get you anywhere. So, you **must** take the tougher route. I say this without question of contradiction. Nothing comes from doing nothing! Or worse than nothing, because the net effect of doing nothing is negative for you and those around you.

As the old saying goes, 'if you want something you don't have, you must do things you're not doing' or 'keep doing what you've always done and you'll keep getting what you've always had'. Take the tougher path and the destination it will be worth the pain, so you must get comfortable with being uncomfortable, or no pain, no gain. Accept it and embrace it - you never know, you might even get to enjoy it!

6. Find a way of including 'it' in your life

This is one of the easiest ways to start the journey. An obvious obstacle is time and money, and these stop people from starting something new. 'I can't leave my job because I have bills to pay'. A valid reason, but not helpful if you want to start a new business with your passion at the heart of it. So, start it in a small way, like enrolling in evening classes or joining a club centred around you chosen path. You'll quickly see the direction of your journey moving towards the desired outcome.

See my section on finding time. You'll find time if you want to. Or you won't, it's up to you.

Example: You want to start your own restaurant, but you can't cook. Start evening cookery classes. Two things will happen. First, you'll meet likeminded people and possibly doors and opportunities will open up to you, and secondly, you'll quickly see if cooking is your passion. All this will be low risk and easily included in your week. Even if you find cooking is not your thing, you would have met some new people, which can't be a bad thing.

7. Design your day

Plan and schedule your day, record the details and make it one of your daily routines (see Rule 4 on habits). The devil is in the detail as the old saying goes, but more importantly, so is the truth. Whether that time spent on tasks - weights lifted, macros eaten, timescales projected, money spent, strength increased etc., the information will give the answer.

Plan everything! Plan your day, plan your work out, plan your meals. Make schedules and lists every day. Then action the plan. Once you've committed your plan to paper, you will be way more likely to achieve it. Also, you will be way more effective too.

There is no downside to designing your day and scheduling your plan of action. None! And believe me, it is a powerful tool to success.

So, record everything and be disciplined in the act. You will see over time that the numbers will change and you can use this information to gauge the next move. This could be increasing, decreasing or pivoting.

Also, keeping a diary (if you can) is a really positive way to record your journey. Diary keeping or 'journaling' is popular at the moment and I would agree this is something that would aid your pursuit of goal achievement.

8. Find likeminded people

If you want to move fast, travel alone. If you want to go far then travel with someone you love. Everyone needs support. It's a very lonely place to try and achieve something significant all alone. It's harder, and in the end, less fulfilling. However, still better to be alone in your relentless approach than to have a destructive outside influence from people who don't want what you want, or show negative responses to your achievements. These people need to be removed from your life, period. We need likeminded people who will celebrate our successes as if they were their own. This will lift us to even greater achievements.

9. Educate yourself on the way

One of the advantages of being dyslexic is that proactive reading is not at the top of my agenda, so I tend to start and then research as I go, using only the information that I think I need, rather than over thinking the process through having too much information.

It will never be the right time, you'll never know enough, so just do it. You can work it out as you go and educate yourself as you move forwards. A huge element of education is experience, it's not just about reading and studying. You will learn skills by approaching the problem and overcoming it. Even if it takes many unsuccessful attempts first.

You'll see from Rule 11 that people put many obstacles in their own way and 'I don't know what I'm doing' is a big one. Guess what, neither does anyone else, so you're no worse off than the next person. So, grunt up and learn it as you go. This book is called *'Sink or Swim'*. Well, you'll only learn to swim if you get in the water. You'll never know what it feels like to actually swim and not sink by reading it in a book. The learning comes from action, from the physical act of jumping into the water and getting fucking wet! Nothing else will help you...nothing! This goes for all aspects of learning. Read all you want, nothing wrong with reading (not my favourite pass time for obvious reasons), but there is no substitute for action. Act, fail, learn. Act, fail less, learn more. Act, achieve, move on. Simple.

10. Back yourself every time

One of my greatest strengths is that I back 'me'. Every time. I never see **impossible**, I see **I'm Possible**! I repeat... 'impossible' is just 'I'm possible' spelt differently. Probably the dyslexic in me. But it's true, my inner strength comes from my unwavering confidence in my ability to adapt to any situation. If you don't back yourself then who will? Your partner (wife, husband) will back you if 'you' think you can do it, but not the reverse. It must come from you. One of the best sayings I've ever heard is this:

> *'He who thinks he can and he who thinks he can't are both usually right.'*

Read that again. There is no more powerful statement for self-belief than this. Period. History is punctuated with stories of the impossible being achieved because someone said 'no, I think I can do that!' - the 4-minute mile, climbing Everest, the motor car, electric light bulb, moon landings... on and on they go. Every single one of these seemingly impossible outcomes at the time were overcome by someone backing themselves first. So, if you take nothing else from this book (there, I've said it again), take rule number 10 and act on it. Back yourself every time. You'll be surprised what happens. The great Gary Player once said, after he shot 63 in a PGA tour event, when asked about the 'lucky' break on 15th hole, 'funny thing is, the harder I work, the luckier I get!' Gary Player backed Gary Player every time and his record speaks for itself. So, start backing you and do the work, the success will come no question, it will just be about when, not if.

11. Don't waste time

I talked earlier about procrastination being the dream killer, and it's true. Doers get there quicker than thinkers, so just start. The biggest obstacle to our own progress is our own 'procrastination' and over thinking, and this comes in many forms:

- It's too hard
- I'm not ready
- I don't have time

- I'm too busy
- I can't afford it
- What will people say?
- I'll just do this first, then I'll start
- I tried it once but it didn't work

On and on we go putting what I call 'start-stops' in our own way, when really if we just set off and keep moving, we will quickly find a way to move forward. You'll work it out as you go, so just starting is the biggest hurdle and after that it's about momentum. But momentum only occurs in nature when there is movement first. *'An object at rest will not gain momentum without first having energy applied.'* This is basic physics 101. So, you apply the energy and the journey can begin.

12. Celebrate small wins

Celebrate the small wins like they're big wins. Be grateful for every little step in the right direction. They will all add up to a great, amazing *'success-full'* journey in the end. This aspect twins with number 7, 'Record everything'. Once you get into the good habit of recording your numbers, whether that's weights, times, reps, scale number, or whatever it is, you'll see the progress, and more importantly it will be measurable progress. This allows you the scope to celebrate the progress at each little milestone.

What do I mean by 'celebrate'? Well, I don't mean throw all the good work out the window by smashing 3 large pizzas. NO! I mean treat yourself to a new gym top or trainers or go to the cinema. But mark the milestone with something that you enjoy or want but wouldn't normally buy or do. It seems obvious, but we often get tied up in the detail of the process and forget to pat ourselves on the back now and again. Be your own cheerleader.

13. Don't Fear 'Fear'

As the great Ian Brown said, 'For everything a reason'. Fear is fear because we make it so. If fear was real then why do some people love sky diving and some get petrified of jumping out of a plane strapped to a small piece of cloth?! It's the same thing, just perceived differently by two different people. You get to decide how you react to the situation, it's your choice. It's not fear, it's your own perception of what makes you scared, so make a different choice and don't be scared. Simply reframe it and change your mindset.

Honestly, I can understand the fear of falling out of a plane because you could actually die, so there is a logic to it. However, the fear of failing is not the same fear. People that are scared of failing are scared of other people's reaction to the situation, not their own. It's an ego thing.

Because, after all it's only failing if you actually give up! So, get up, grunt up, brush yourself off and go again, because trust me, no one cares if you fall down…no one (apart from your mother, perhaps)!

Plus, nothing worth having in life comes quickly or easily. Furthermore, no one teaches you how to get up and try again that is on you 100%. So, buck up, Princess.

14. Lastly, have some fucking fun

Life is for living, that's what they say, and for the most part that's true, but don't forget to have some fun whilst you're living! Living life to the full doesn't always mean fun, it can be hard, painful, stressful and/or uncomfortable. These are not adjectives you would associate with the word 'fun', but trust me, sometimes the most enjoyment you can have comes from overcoming adversity.

That being said, you still need to have the traditional types of fun too, so sometimes get off the train of life and do some sight-seeing and play for a while. You can always get back on and be 'relentless and driven' again once you've had some down time.

You'd be amazed how many people get stressed about actually enjoying themselves. What's the point in that? Focus on you and do what you want for once, then you'll be in a much better position to help others and give your partner or family the time they need, without feeling like it's all on you. So, chill for a bit.

One of the best ways to ensure you have an enjoyable life is to break it down into the days and weeks first. What I mean by that is 'Design your day' (see Rules 6 and 7), when you plan your day how you want it, then you can fill it with productive periods (those things that must be done), reactive periods (those periods to which other people need you to get things done for them), plus a period of down time or fun time.

I have a learning hour in my working day. I set down all my work devices and listen to a TED talk or a podcast. I find it not only increases my knowledge base, but it also energises me to get the work done after the learning hour. It's a win-win in my view.

You decide, but the most important thing is that if you 'design your day' make it one you'd want to have (it is in your gift). Plus, if you do it, even in a small way, it makes life so much better.

Side Note: 'life is a balancing act'

Anyone who tells you to get a 'life/work balance' is talking shit. No, I'm not joking! They are well meaning, but, in my view, they don't understand how the system called life works. So, please do not listen to 'life coaches' or 'gurus' who suggest that your issue is a life/work balance issue. Your issue is a life issue and work is just part of the whole thing, not something that sits outside of everything else you do.

Let me explain. 'Work' is part of life, just as relationships, fun, sport and relaxing are part of life. To suggest that work and life are opposite ends of a scale of happiness is just rubbish. Life is the scale! Happiness is not measured by how little 'work' you do verses how much 'life' you do.

I know many people who love their work and love getting up on a Monday morning to start the day that they have designed. Please don't tell me they should stop doing what they love to conform with society's version of life/work/play equation.

I love what I do for a living and my work is part of the fabric of my life, not an opposing force taking all the fun away. I think what people want to say is 'life needs balance', and the component parts include love, work, relaxation, fun, socialising, sport, exercise, eating, drinking, education, relationships, being wild, and being quiet or still. All of these are LIFE. It's like the scales of justice with the lady holding the scale being 'LIFE', and all the parts of the fabric of life are in the bowls. You decide what makes that balanced.

What I would say is that if you hate Mondays or fear going to work then that needs changing. My brother once told me that 'if you make your business something you love, you'll never work a day in your life'. Great advice (don't tell him that though!).

To find true happiness in life you need to have meaning and purpose, and you need to have action and movement in that direction. Working and contributing to society is part of that equation. So, the answer is to find work that you are passionate about, which gives your life meaning and direction. If that work serves to help others then then that's a positive gain for everyone. Make Mondays amazing.

APPLYING THE SYSTEM

So how do we actually apply the system? The 14-point blueprint above sets out the key fundamentals for achieving an end goal. The key to achieving your goals and applying the system is a 'Growth Mindset', and to be open minded to the process.

I love analogies for explaining things, so here are a few to explain how the system works. Generally, they are common sense (but the trouble with common sense, I hear you shout, is that it's not very common)!

EXAMPLES:

Example 1 - You want healthy teeth when you're in you 80's? Brush and floss your teeth every day for eighty years!

Obviously, you can't brush your teeth 75,000 (the average amount of brushing in an 80-year life span of someone who's kept all their teeth) times in one go, or just visit the dentist to check your teeth each year, these alone will not achieve the desired outcome or goal. Your teeth will rot or you'll brush them away. Either way, you're now sucking on soft fruit and spooning down baby food with your teeth in a glass by your bed.

Brushing them once in isolation does absolutely nothing, but it's the small twice-a-day habit of brushing and flossing that keeps them healthy.

Example 2 - You want to get fit and loose 2 stone in 6 months?

Go to the gym 4 times a week and eat less than you burn every day for 28 weeks. A systematic approach to calorie deficit and exercise to loosing 1 lb per week for 28 weeks will achieve the goal.

Randomly starting to eat vegetable soup, juicing, and trying those skinny jeans on every month and hoping after 6 tries that they'll eventually fit will not work!

Example 3 - You want to write a book?

Commit to writing a page of 100 words a day for a year. After 365 days, voilà - a book (that's going to be approx. 36,500 words)!

Just thinking about it and talking about your book or booking a meeting with a publisher to discuss your idea, is not going to make it happen. One page a day for a year might be enough to get yourself published.

Hopefully you get the idea. These are only a small selection of very short examples of daily habit forming to achieve a goal that requires you to focus on the daily habits, not the end result. The outcome will be a by-product of the good habits, therefore, look after the daily habits and the end result will take care of itself.

MY VALUE STRUCTURE

Finding your 'WHY' or your passion is tough, but knowing what your core values are is a good place to start. Your own personal value structure is the foundation of who you are and a key component or framework for you find your passion in life.

Please don't mistake this for how some large companies and organisations have set out their 'Core Values' and often post them up on the wall. Generally, these are just stale 'non sensical, no brainer' statements that are pretty much elements of life that are, or at least should be, a 'given'. In my opinion these are not values.

For example, you will see a business offering their core values as being 'Flexible, Reliable, Honest and acting with Integrity'. I would question why you'd need to tell people that they are honest or that they act with integrity. I would suggest this is just stating the fucking obvious. Your core values need to be aligned with what you see as values that are fundamental to you being you as a person. What makes you, 'you'.

The following are what I see as my core values, to give you an idea of what I'm suggesting you look for in you. It's a good place to start.

My Core Values are:

1. **Happiness first**

    My decisions are based on my happiness or the happiness of the people I love.

2. **I back me**

    At every turn or junction in life, I back me. Every time!

3. **I look for the positive**

    I find the positives and learn the lessons from all difficult situations (I reframe it).

4. **I take responsibility**

    If I fuck up, I hold my hands up and take responsibility for my actions.

5. **I get back up**
   If I fall, I get right back up.

Side note: My definition of 'happiness' (as I see it anyway) is the purpose and meaning to my life, the reason I get up every day, the feeling I get as I move forward towards my goal. Happiness is a state of mind derived from the process, not the destination. The best way to describe what makes me happy is the journey, not the end itself. When I get to the end I usually say 'ok, what now?!' and start immediately looking for the next challenge. So, I know it's not the prize at the end that floats my boat. This may be different for you.

I do, however, think people most confuse a momentary state of joy with true happiness. Happiness, and more importantly true happiness, is all encompassing. This only comes from having meaning and purpose in life. This happens when you take responsibility for your life and move forwards on the right path (your path). You must, therefore, find your path and the purpose that gives your life meaning, and happiness will be a by-product.

In short, happiness is the outcome from doing what allows you to take ownership of your life's direction.

Section 11
Curve Ball Thought

In my opinion (and I'm no expert), 'Self Help' as a genre is somewhat hypocritical and contradictory. For the industry to survive, it requires *us* to be forever searching for the next big thing. The next guru to show us the path to redemption, fulfilment and/or personal happiness.

Obviously, I'm not suggesting that this book should not be placed in such a category (it most probably will). However, it does seem slightly ironic that you need to read someone else's book on a 'how-to' subject to gain information on 'how to help yourself'. By definition you are not 'helping' yourself, you are seeking guidance and help from others. True self help comes from the internal space, not from external stimulation. I think this re-direction comes from the fact that people don't naturally like or want to ask for help. So, we re-frame this as 'self-help' to make it more palatable. We are helping ourselves, not asking for help. I'm sorry, but you are asking for help, and that's ok! So, I would like to (as postscript) offer this small re-directional, re-framing, advice on the subject.

You've now (hopefully) read the story section of this book, and the moral tales that set out the blueprint for my system, and I hope you've enjoyed it. However, I would ask you to consider the characters from the story in reverse. What I mean by that is imagine Gruff as the lead character of my system, not Adam. If you place the learning outcomes from Gruff's perspective, they hold far greater meaning. So, what am I asking or suggesting? Well in short, 'help' others. Place your energy in the direction of the service and support of other people's needs, other than your own (as Gruff has).

Be the teacher, not the student of your own life. Set the lessons and deliver the message to others for them to learn. Lead by example, then you will see the true essence of self-help. Use your 'self' to 'help' others. It's in the service and support of others that we will find true fulfilment and true happiness. It has been said that the best way to really know a subject is to teach it to someone else. I believe this to be true. Moreover, the best way to know yourself is to help someone else on their journey.

Section 12

Final Thoughts

As I promised, I'll tell you how it turned out for me. Well, I'm still failing, falling, leaping and jumping. I still struggle with the reading and writing bit, but that's just how it is. This book has shown me that I can get over my inabilities by using my abilities.

My dyslexia never defined me, but it has shaped me, no doubt. I know how to understand it and re-direct it in a positive way. It's become something I just accept as part of the fabric of me. My brain functions the way it does and having a system to control the chaos is vital to my ability to move forward. I enjoy the processes more than the end result. I will continue to progress the changes in my life and enjoy the ride.

This book has taken me on a path that I didn't know it would when I started a year ago. As I have put my ideas down on paper, new ideas have been created. So a bit like my 'Get Fit For 50' campaign, I think this may also push me I another direction. Danny Stimson, published author, has a nice ring to it.

I have my system, value structure and a natural growth mindset, and that is what makes me 'me'. I know this book won't be for everyone, I fully understand and accept that, but it's my book. When I set out to write it I gave myself one year and I have achieved that goal, so by definition I know the 14-point blueprint works.

More importantly, the book is, in principle, how I function, so it has contextualised what helps me to achieve my goals, and that is what I set out to do when I committed to write it. If it helps others then great, if not, I truly don't really care.

I haven't got it all worked out by any stretch of imagination. I'm still trying to work it out on the way, but, I know what the finish looks like for each small journey I make. Who knows what the final destination will be, but with a planned approach, here's hoping it will be to my liking, and most importantly, I have an amazing companion for the ride.

Lastly, 'time is valuable' so thank you for taking some time out of your day to read or listen to this book. Please pass the book on to anyone who you think is struggling with where they are in life and might need a push. I'm not suggesting this is the answer, but hopefully in a small way it may nudge them in the right direction. I wish you luck and love on your path... just make sure it's the right path, your path and obviously, have some fucking fun on the way.

STOICISM LESSONS AND WISDOM

Stoicism is a philosophy that resonates very strongly in my mind, but for most people, when you mention Stoicism or being 'stoic', they think of being stern or dour, and strict and unwavering. This is partly true, but for those who don't know, The Stoics were intense thinkers and the lessons that have been credited to stoicism are reliable life lessons. The Stoics, far from being stern, dull and unpassionate, actually created their philosophy system to achieve lifelong happiness.

The following list is only a snippet of the stoic lessons and philosophies. As you will see, there is a strong relatable thread between my system and the stoic lessons. So, it's not a coincidence that the philosophy resonates strongly in my mind and has reinforced my own mindset as I've read more on the writings and teachings of Stoics like Seneca, Epictetus, and Marcus Aurelius, among others.

Stoics lessons

1. Do things that are difficult. It will make you stronger, mentally and emotionally.
2. 3-point assessment of actions – motivation, emotion, pro-action or reaction = outcome.
3. Awareness of thought - be mindful of your own thoughts.
4. Kindness to others – in the service of others.
5. Act with Passion – find your 'why'.
6. Keep the 'end' in mind – visualisation.
7. Perseverance and daily application – routine.

As you can hopefully see, the above seven-point list (not exhaustive) hits a number of marks in respect of my system, like habits, passion, visualisation, etc.

Other thoughts

This short passage is just to show you how people with a limited, closed mindset think, and conversely how, generally, the reverse growth mindset is the more productive mindset. If you've ever said any of the following then you know what I'm talking about.

1. I'll jump when I learn how to fly!
    - You'll only learn how to fly if you jump!
    - You'll never be ready so just do it! If you wait till you are ready you'll never start.

2. I'll be happy when I get there!
   - You'll only get there when you're happy!
   - Happiness is a state of mind not a thing, a place, a job or a salary. It is how you feel about these things. A Casio watch tells the same time as a Rolex watch. A Ferrari drives on the same road as a Mini. Does it make the views on the journey better? (ok, maybe quicker but they're the same views!)
3. I'll only believe it when I see it!
   - You'll only see it once you believe it!
   - Some people think this is question of faith. Well, guess what, they are right, but not faith in a higher power, God or a religion, but faith in yourself, faith in your ability. So, take that leap of faith and see if you can fly!
4. It's not my fault!
   - It is! Deal with it!
   - Once you take responsibility for who you are, and where you are in life, you will be able to move on. Otherwise, you'll stay exactly where you are and be resentful, which is not a positive state of mind.
5. I'm not where I want to be in life.
   - You are exactly where you are meant to be.
   - I've said it already, but 'of the things in life you can control, you get what you deserve,' enough said.

So, what now?

By way of a conclusion, I thought it would help to try and contextualise what you can do now to move the needle of your own life. The following paragraph is, in my view, an abridged summary of the book, and is what you need to do if you want to make that change. I hope it helps.

- Firstly, look at where you are currently in life and now imagine the perfect version of your life. What would that look like?
- Then imagine the worst outcome and a life that is painful, sad and tragic. I'm assuming you are nowhere near the second version. Right?
- Now, take full responsibility for where you are currently.
- Find some motivation and passion for what would drive you towards the first version of your life.
- Now make a plan (design your day) on how to get it embedded into your everyday life.
- Action the plan by making small changes to your daily habits to move you in the right direction.
- Be relentless in this pursuit and be consistent in your approach.
- Plus, have some fun on the way.
- The rest is up to you.......

I wish you love and luck for the next chapter in your life.

So, is it sink, or is it swim? It's up to you!

Section 13

Quotes I Love

This additional short section of the book is a list of some of my favourite quotes from books, inspirational speakers and films. Please take them for yourself and read them over and over again. They will inspire you, trust me. Or even better, read the books, listen to the speakers or watch the films.

1. Impossible is really 'I'm possible' spelt differently.
2. Get comfortable with being uncomfortable.
3. Your biggest mistake in life will be avoiding making mistakes.
4. See it, believe it, achieve it – Napoleon Hill's classic
5. If you think you can, or you think you can't, you are probably right.
6. Be mindful of your self-talk; be nice, be positive, be clear.
7. I love it when a plan comes together – *The A-Team*
8. It's not how hard you can hit, it's how hard can you get hit and keep moving forward - *Rocky V*
9. Sometimes Joel, ya just gotta say 'what the Fuck' - *Risky Business*

10. Life moves pretty fast so ya gotta stop and look around or ya might miss something – *Ferris Bueller's Day Off*
11. Inch by inch...the inches we need are all around us in every break in the game – *Any Given Sunday*
12. Life ain't all sunshine and rainbows. It's a very mean and nasty place and it will beat you to your knees if you let it - *Rocky V*
13. Pain is temporary. Eventually it will be replaced by something else. If I quit, however, it will last forever - Lance Armstrong

I thought I should have 14 quotes so lastly, and the most powerful:

14. Our greatest fear is not that we are inadequate, but that we are powerful beyond measure - Marianne Williamson

Section 14
Your Next Chapter

This is your blank page, to write your next chapter. Is it sink or is it swim? It's on you!

About the Author

My name is Daniel (most people call me Danny) I was born May 6th 1967 in a Naval Hospital in Mauritius (an Island in the in the Indian Ocean).

I'm a 'middle child' (those that know .....know!)

I was diagnosed Dyslexic aged 8 in 1975.

This is my first, and probably my last book. It took me a year to write during the 2nd Covid Pandemic of 2021.

My working history over the last 40 years looks like this:

I'm a qualified Stone Mason, I served a 3-year apprenticeship with English Heritage during the Mid/late 80's, then became a stone carver and sculptor. I've been a Buyer and estimator for a construction company in the Mid 90's, I retrained as a surveyor during the 00's and became a director of an Architectural firm. I've been a director of a construction firm; ran my own stone carving workshop teaching the art of stone carving and, pre Covid during 2018/19, ran the Fit mindset Code health and well-being business. Currently (since 2014) I now run my own Construction Surveying business.

Also during last 20 or so years I've been commissioned to Carve around eight public and private sculptures, also I've qualified as UEFA B license football Coach and competed in a men's physique body building competition (at 52), I'm a 6 handicap Golfer and I'm not done yet!

Oh and lastly I'm a husband to the girl I married 30 odd years ago, a father of two and a proud grandad of one.

If you want to reach out and get in touch – Email me: ***dan67stim@gmail.com***